MILLY

AND THE SHAWL OF ATHENA

The First of Many Adventures

J P Allen

J P Allen

Dedication

To all the mums and dads that inspire, nurture and protect us.

iii

Acknowledgement

Thank you mum for telling me so many stories and fuelling my love of adventure, fiction and fantasy.

Also big thanks to my family and you the readers for supporting me in my writing journey.

Table of Contents

Prelude

In the quiet depths of time, where minutes merged with aeons, stood a forgotten temple. This sacred site held secrets whispered only by the winds, which danced through the temple's marble columns and rustled the leaves of ancient olive trees. At its heart, in a chamber bathed in the warm glow of flickering flames, hung a pure white cloth woven with threads of shimmering gold. Legends said this cloth was Athena's Shawl — an artefact of extraordinary power, believed to be a remnant of a mystical force predating the very concept of time itself.

Within the ancient temple, a sacred ritual had been passed down through generations, entrusted only to the most esteemed priests and priestesses. The ceremony began with whispered invocations to Athena, seeking her blessing and wisdom in times of war and unrest. As the fire roared, the priests and priestesses performed the Ritual of Athena's Shawl, casting their shadows upon the cloth. These shadows, intricate and ethereal, leapt and twirled, creating a living tapestry of sorts. As the flames danced, so too did the stories of the past, present, and future.

Each flicker of the flames breathed life into the tales woven into the sacred ritual, projecting onto the cloth the deeds of gods and mortals alike. The shadowy figures on Athena's Shawl enacted battles against monstrous foes, embarked on epic adventures, and unravelled the mysteries of the cosmos. The cloth seemed to absorb the very essence of the stories being told, mesmerising its worshippers. Yet, despite their curiosity, the priests and priestesses dared not touch Athena's Shawl. None knew what might happen if they did.

The guardians of the temple, inspired by the wisdom of the goddess Athena, had watched over the shawl for countless generations. The golden threads were imbued with the essence of ancient magic, connecting the temple to a realm beyond mortal comprehension. For centuries, this temple had been a haven of peace and reverence. Yet, hidden within the shadows lurked Deimos Asgard, an evil priest whose very name sent shivers down the spines of the locals. His malevolent schemes threatened to shatter the serenity that had long cloaked the temple.

One fateful day, a horde of invaders stormed the temple, and the village nestled at its foothills became embroiled in the chaos of war. Deimos Asgard, who had coveted the mystic white cloth for years, seized this opportunity to enact his dark plans. Amid the turmoil, the sinister priest — clad in black robes and wearing a purple amulet that pulsed with the essence of dark magic — made his way to the chamber where Athena's Shawl hung before the great flame. There, blocking his path, stood the Sphinx: a formidable beast with the body of a lion, the wings of a bird, and the head of a woman.

Deimos Asgard, a master of riddles, shared a peculiar relationship with the Sphinx. She had unwittingly fallen in love with him, and he cunningly used this to his advantage. Though entrusted to guard Athena's Shawl, the Sphinx's loyalty lay with him, and she swore to do his bidding. The sound of clashing swords echoed nearby, growing louder by the minute. Deimos, anxious, removed his dark amulet and handed it to the Sphinx, who held the chain delicately between her teeth.

"Take my amulet, Sphinx," he commanded. "Hide it well and guard it with your best riddle. Its power is beyond comprehension, and I cannot risk it being found."

The Sphinx nodded, then bounded gracefully down a shadowy corridor with the amulet clutched between her teeth. Deimos Asgard stepped into the sacred chamber where Athena's Shawl hung before the fierce, roaring flames. He had performed the ritual countless times with evil intent, but this was the moment he had waited for. His shadow, long and twisted, stretched across the shimmering cloth.

"Finally!" he exclaimed. As his fingers brushed against the fabric, a deafening crash signalled the invaders breaching the temple walls.

Deimos found himself face to face with the blade of an enormous axe, wielded by a towering warrior. Instinctively, he clutched the corner of Athena's Shawl. To his shock, the cloth quivered and undulated under his touch. Suddenly, the priest was pulled into its silken folds, vanishing entirely from the mortal realm.

In the chaos, his loyal acolytes launched a desperate counterattack against the invaders. But as Deimos disappeared, Athena's Shawl, infused with his frantic magic, flickered and vanished as well, leaving the villagers and temple guardians bewildered. The once-glimmering golden threads, radiant as starlight, were gone, leaving the temple defenceless against the encroaching darkness.

In the aftermath, despair gripped the village. The absence of Athena's Shawl stripped the temple of its spiritual protection, leaving it vulnerable. The surrounding woods seemed to mourn, echoing with the sorrowful cries of guardian spirits now bound by hopelessness.

Huddled in whispered circles, the villagers debated their fate. Rumours spread that Deimos had stolen the mystical cloth, intending to wield its ancient powers for domination—not just over the village, but perhaps the entire world. The elders speculated that the guardian spirits, in a final act of defiance, had sent the shawl elsewhere to prevent it from falling into his hands.

Confusion and fear settled over the village. Their only hope lay in recovering the lost relic, but the question haunted them: where was Athena's Shawl, and what had become of Deimos Asgard?

Chapter 1
The King Isn't Dead, Long Live

The sun hung low in the sky, casting long shadows across the vibrant landscape. Four warriors, clad in intricate, gleaming armour, crouched behind moss-covered ruins in an overgrown forest. They were a formidable squad, united in their quest, their faces hidden beneath polished helmets. Their fearless leader, Captain Catalina, surveyed the horizon with steely resolve. Their mission was simple yet crucial: infiltrate the enemy stronghold and free their captive king. Tension hung thick in the air — the calm before the storm.

"Stay sharp, everyone," Captain Catalina commanded, her voice steady and resolute. "Our success today determines the fate of our kingdom."

Her warriors — a team of ancient English and French knights — nodded in silent agreement. Among them were Wolfstan, the swift and agile archer; Mirabel, the master tactician; and Faramund, the valiant and mighty warrior. With synchronised precision, they melted into the shadows, advancing towards the enemy's fortress. The sun dipped lower, casting an ethereal glow over the sandstone walls that loomed ahead. Catalina suddenly raised her hand, signalling the team to halt.

They froze, staring at the distant towers, then at their captain, awaiting her command. "The King is somewhere in there," she whispered, her eyes narrowing as she studied the fortress. "We must move swiftly and silently."

As they approached, the rhythmic beat of drums filled the air, mingling with the distant clang of armour. The fortress gates loomed above them, an imposing barrier to their mission's success. Wolfstan, arrow notched and ready, scanned the walls for a weak point. "There,

Captain," he murmured, pointing to a weathered section of stone. "I can create a distraction."

Catalina nodded. Wolfstan stepped forward, drawing his bowstring with practised ease. In one fluid motion, he released an arrow, striking the wall with a resonant thud. A nearby guard turned towards the sound and left his post to investigate. Seizing the moment, Catalina signalled her squad to move. They slipped through the partially opened gates like shadows, their hearts pounding as they ventured deeper into enemy territory.

The labyrinthine corridors challenged their resolve, but the warriors pressed on, overcoming obstacles through teamwork and determination. After dispatching a horde of enemy soldiers, they stumbled upon a large treasure chest hidden in the corner of a dimly lit room. Mirabel opened it, revealing nothing but a tiny key. She retrieved it and handed it to Catalina.

"Perhaps this is the key to freeing King Jason from his shackles," Mirabel suggested.

"Nice work, Mirabel," Catalina said, examining the key. "This must be what those soldiers were guarding."

At last, they reached the chamber where King Jason III was imprisoned. His eyes widened with hope as the warriors entered. The shackles on his wrists glinted faintly in the dim light. Catalina approached him with a triumphant smile.

"We've come for you, Your Majesty," she declared, unlocking the restraints with the key Mirabel had found.

The King, his gratitude unmistakable, nodded to his rescuers. "You have my eternal thanks, brave warriors. Our kingdom is forever in your debt."

As the squad began escorting him to safety, a radiant light suddenly enveloped the chamber.

"Milly? Milly!"

The world around them dissolved, pixel by pixel. The warriors, once heroic figures of flesh and blood, transformed into avatars on a computer screen.

"Great job, guys!" Milly said through her headset, her voice brimming with excitement. She had chosen to play as Wolfstan, as usual. Ashley played as Mirabel, while Lucy took on the role of Faramund. With their friends Harry and Chris unavailable to play as Captain Catalina or King Jason, the game's AI had filled the roles seamlessly.

"Now," Milly continued, "we just have to get King Jason home safely."

"Should be interesting," Ashley said. "King Jason is a bit of a clown."

"So true," Lucy agreed. "You've got to wonder what they want with such a useless old man."

"What are you doing?" Milly's younger sister, Francesca—known as Fran to her friends—knocked on the locked bedroom door.

"I have to go," Milly told her friends. "But we'll play tomorrow, yeah?" She said her goodbyes, took off her headset, and exited *War of the Ages 2*. "I'm playing my game, Fran! What do you want?"

"Dad says dinner's ready," Fran replied. "He says, 'Get down here now, miss!'"

"Yeah, yeah," Milly muttered, rolling her eyes. "I'll be right there." She knew her dad was probably being playful, but she wasn't in the mood to test his patience. Since her mother had gone missing, he had been distant—not cruel, but distant. There was always a faraway look in

6

his eyes, as though he were trying to solve an unsolvable puzzle. Her mother, Louise Martin, was the puzzle's most glaring missing piece. Both father and daughter wanted nothing more than to find her, but neither knew where to start.

Milly shut off her computer and made her way downstairs. Her younger brother, Charlie, had just finished setting the table, and their nine-month-old Cavalier King Charles Spaniel, Louie, sat expectantly at their father's feet.

"Not today, boy," John Martin said, placing a steaming shepherd's pie on the table. "You've already had your dinner, of your favourite Louie chewies"

Louie huffed in protest and padded away, his long, ruddy brown ears nearly brushing the floor. Milly often wondered how he managed not to trip over them. The dog settled under the table as Milly and Fran sat across from Charlie.

"We had a lesson on the Second World War yesterday," Charlie said as he unfolded his napkin. "Wasn't Grandpa talking about his dad being involved?"

"That was a long time ago," their father replied. "He told me his dad served in Europe and was involved in the Mediterranean conflict. But he didn't talk much about it." John's tone grew wistful, his thoughts drifting to conversations he'd once shared with Louise and her father.

"Come to think of it," Charlie said, turning to his sister, "were you playing that war game again? When do I get a turn?"

"*War of the Ages* is too scary for a little kid like you," Milly said matter-of-factly. "And it's my computer. I bought it with my own money."

"That's not fair!" Charlie protested, folding his arms. "Dad, tell her she should give me a turn!"

John cracked a faint smile as he served Charlie some shepherd's pie. "That's your sister's choice. It's her computer. If you save up your allowance, maybe you can buy your own."

"Mum didn't let me buy my own computer until this year," Milly pointed out, shooting her brother a knowing look. The comment carried an edge, a subtle jab at the rules she'd had to follow. "I wasn't even allowed to play computer games until recently. The same rules should apply to him."

"Well, yeah," her father replied. "Those were your mother's rules, and we'll be sticking to them. When Charlie turns twelve, he can buy his own computer if he wants."

"Aw, Dad. Okay," Charlie said, sulking briefly before digging into his dinner. Then his face lit up. "Hey, Dad! Did you know I got full marks on my spelling test today?"

Charlie absolutely adored his father. That was fine, but Milly couldn't help thinking he was sucking up a bit. She also had a sneaking suspicion he had a crush on her best friend, Ashley, despite only being eight years old. Their mother used to call him a "little ladies' man." Whatever that meant.

"You told me," John Martin said, swallowing a bite of shepherd's pie. "You must have worked hard, even with football practice keeping you busy." He turned to Milly. "You could take a leaf out of Charlie's book, you know. Your grades haven't been the best lately."

Milly raised an eyebrow but didn't respond. She took a deliberate bite of shepherd's pie, ignoring him. Whatever, she thought. As if I can focus on grades with everything that's going on.

Charlie beamed, launching into a rambling account of how he was going to win the spelling bee, become the best football player in school, and accomplish a million other ambitious goals. Milly couldn't

8

understand how someone so young managed to keep his dreams so neatly organised.

"I'm going to tell Mum you were bragging, Charlie," Fran said suddenly.

Fran was nine years old and a notorious tattletale.

"How exactly are you going to do that?" Milly snapped before she could stop herself.

The room fell uncomfortably silent. Fran froze, her fork halfway to her mouth.

Milly immediately regretted saying it, but a part of her wished someone would just say it outright. Mum had been missing for months. For all they knew, she could be dead in a ditch somewhere. Milly hated thinking that, but the thought lingered. Worse, she sometimes wondered if their mother wasn't really missing. What if Dad was lying about the police looking for her? Why didn't he go searching himself?

A horrible thought clawed its way into her mind: *What if Mum left us? What if she doesn't love us anymore?*

Milly shook her head, trying to banish the idea. *No, that can't be true.* Sure, Mum drank a bit, but she'd always seemed happy. She wouldn't just leave... right?

She reached down to stroke Louie, who was curled up under the table and handed him a Louie chewie. His soft fur and little whimper of contentment comforted her as she tried to keep her emotions in check.

Fran pushed her plate away and rested her head in her hands. "I really miss her," she said softly. "Have the police found anything out, Dad?"

"Not yet," John said, his voice heavy. "But they're going to find her. I promise."

"How do you know that?" Milly blurted out, her hand freezing mid-stroke.

Her father shot her a sharp look that said *not in front of the kids*.

Milly sighed and cleared her throat. "Sorry. Uh… does anyone want tea?"

She stood abruptly, grabbing the teapot, and Louie trotted after her hoping for another treat. She busied herself in the kitchen, the kettle's low rumble masking the chatter at the table.

Milly often fantasised about escaping her complicated life and living in simpler times — maybe as a mediaeval knight like Wolfstan in *War of the Ages 2*. Life would be straightforward: fighting battles, saving the day, and capping it all off with a slice of pie and a Red Bull at the local tavern.

Wait. Did they even have Red Bull in mediaeval times?

She frowned at the thought, then chuckled lightly. Louie pawed at her leg, his big eyes begging for a treat. "Alright, boy," she said, reaching into the treat jar and handing him two Louie chewies. He crunched them loudly, and for a moment, his happiness made hers feel a little less out of reach.

After dinner and a spot of tea, Charlie volunteered to help his father with the washing-up. Fran went outside to play skipping with the neighbour's daughter, while Milly—her mind still swirling with troubling thoughts of her mother's disappearance—crept upstairs to her parents' bedroom. She opened the door as quietly as she could and tiptoed inside. She hadn't been in the room for ages—not since before her mother had gone. It looked much the same as it had before, albeit a little messier. The unmade bed sagged like a frown, and the bedside table was cluttered with empty coffee cups.

Milly closed the door softly behind her. For some reason, she felt drawn to her mother's wardrobe. Her mother hadn't been posh, exactly, but she had a wonderful sense of style. Seeing the wardrobe still full of her dresses, coats, and cardigans gave Milly a flicker of hope that her mother hadn't left by choice. Her mother had adored her clothes, and perhaps even more, her Tiffany jewellery. Surely, she wouldn't have abandoned those. But this realisation also filled Milly with dread. It confirmed what she'd been trying not to admit—her mother was truly missing. Tears pricked her eyes as she sifted through the familiar garments. Her mother's favourite blouse—the blue one with the white buttons—still carried the faint scent of her strawberry perfume.

Just then, the door moved slightly, and Milly's heart lifted when she saw Louie enter. Sensing her distress, he leapt up and nuzzled her, offering the comfort she needed.

As Milly wiped her tears with the back of her hand, something in the far corner of the wardrobe caught her eye. It was bunched up oddly. That's strange, she thought. Mum always hangs her clothes. She reached down to pick it up, and it unfurled in her hands—a delicate white cloth, embroidered with golden threads.

"What is this?" she murmured, her brow furrowing. A wave of déjà vu washed over her. "This looks like…" She racked her brain, trying to place the memory. "But… there's no way." Closing her eyes, she let the memory surface. Mr Hayes's classroom, on a dreary day, several months ago…

"Imagine, if you will," Milly's history teacher, Mr Hayes, began, *"a forgotten temple in Ancient Greece, sometime towards the end of the 1st century. This temple held secrets that resonated through the ages. Legends spoke of a pure white cloth, woven with threads of gold, known as Athena's Shawl. It was believed to possess extraordinary powers… but*

11

even those who protected and worshipped Athena's Shawl didn't know exactly how these powers worked."

"What sort of powers did it have?" Ashley blurted out. She had a habit of forgetting to raise her hand before speaking in class, which often got her into trouble with other teachers—but not Mr Hayes.

"Hold your horses, Miss Harris," Mr Hayes said. "I'm getting there. Now..." he continued, "imagine brave warriors clad in shining armour, defending the honour of their kingdoms. In our tale, these noble cavalrymen find themselves entangled with the secrets of the ancient temple and the elusive Athena's Shawl."

Milly's mind painted vivid images of bronze-armoured soldiers on horseback, their swords gleaming in the sunlight. She feverishly took notes as Mr Hayes spoke and thought of Wolfstan from War of the Ages 2, drawing his bowstring, squinting, and always searching for weak spots in the enemy's defences.

"These cavalrymen weren't so noble in the eyes of the priests and priestesses who watched over Athena's Shawl at the temple, though..." Mr Hayes paused to sift through the papers on his desk. It wasn't often he had to check his notes, but, being relatively new to teaching, his students gave him grace whenever he did. "Their king was a greedy man, and he became rather obsessed with getting his hands on Athena's Shawl. He sent his best fighters to retrieve it for him, which led to the temple being raided and the nearby village pillaged."

Milly raised her hand, a question burning at the back of her mind.

"Yes, Miss Martin?"

"So... the cavalrymen were the bad guys?"

Mr Hayes smiled. "Well," he said, "in this story, there are no good or bad guys. Both sides were doing what they thought was right. Not everything is black and white, Amelia. Remember that." He always *used Milly's full name in class. Turning to address the rest of the students, he added, "In fact, you'd all do well to remember this while writing your essays, which are due when?" He gave Harry a pointed look, as though testing him.*

"Er..." Harry wracked his brain. "Um... Fr—"

"Friday. Exactly," Mr Hayes said. The class giggled, and Harry hung his head, slightly embarrassed.

Mr Hayes made the "silent fox" hand signal, pressing his middle fingers to his thumb and holding up his pinky and index finger. The class quietened, and he cleared his throat. "Earlier, Miss Harris asked what sort of powers Athena's Shawl possessed." Almost every student leaned forward, eager to learn more about the legendary shawl with magical powers. "Unfortunately," Mr Hayes said, "I don't know the answer. No one truly understood the powers of Athena's Shawl, likely because it disappeared before anyone could study it properly."

"But, Mr Hayes," Ashley said, frantically waving her hand in the air, "how did it disappear? And why? Where is it?"

"That's the thing," Mr Hayes replied. "It's a bit of a mystery. Keep in mind, though, that there's no such thing as magic. Athena's Shawl was simply an artefact important to the Ancient Greeks. The legend surrounding it is very likely nothing more than a myth. The Ancient Greeks loved their mythology, after all!"

At that moment, the bell rang, and the students began packing up their belongings.

"Your essays are due on Friday!" Mr Hayes called out. "Come and see me if you have any questions!"

Milly snapped out of it, thinking, *Yeah, right... as if Athena's Shawl would be crumpled up in Mum's closet.* She examined it again, running her fingers over the soft, silky fabric. It wasn't like anything she'd ever seen her mother wear. *Maybe I'll ask Dad about it later,* she thought. Still, she wasn't sure her dad would appreciate her snooping in his bedroom, so she stuffed the cloth into her trouser pocket and slinked back to her room.

Chapter 2
The Cloth

Milly wasn't entirely sure what to do with the cloth. She wasn't even certain why she'd taken it from her mother's closet in the first place. Perhaps she was drawn to the beautiful golden threads, or maybe — and this particular thought made her feel like she was losing the plot — she'd felt the cloth calling to her in some strange way. Whatever it was about the cloth, it comforted her. It made her feel connected to her mother somehow.

The next morning, before heading off to school with Fran and Charlie, she tucked the cloth beneath her pillow. She'd decided she didn't want anyone to know about it, not even her father. Not yet, anyway.

She put on her school uniform and tied her long brown hair back into a ponytail. Looking at herself in the full-length mirror propped against the wall beside her dresser, she clipped her grown-out fringe to the sides of her head with several blue barrettes.

"I wonder if Harry will eat lunch with us today," she said aloud. Harry O'Leary was the Irish boy in Milly and Ashley's history class. He'd been held back a year, so he was thirteen and, in Milly's opinion, quite handsome. He was something of a sports hero at their school, which Milly found inspiring. Although she did fairly well in school — particularly in music, history, and maths — she sometimes wished she could focus more on sports, especially hockey and netball.

Netball season was only just starting, and Milly, as captain of the school's netball team, was excited to see how the new recruits would perform. She'd finally convinced her friend Ashley to join the team, which had been no small feat, as Ashley wasn't keen on running around and getting sweaty. She much-preferred shopping or playing chess against Harry — not just because she always beat him, but because she was exceptionally skilled at it.

"I want to hang out with you and Lucy more, though," Ashley had told Milly. "I feel like I never really get to talk to you guys, except at school and when we play *War of the Ages*."

"So?" Lucy waggled her eyebrows at Ashley. "Join the netball team! It's fun once you get the hang of it."

"That's a great idea!" Milly said. "We could honestly use more players who are good at strategising, Ash."

"Alright, well… you'd better teach me how to play the stupid game, then," Ashley said. "And I'm not quitting the chess team."

While Milly was pondering this, Fran barged into her room.

"Um, hello?" Milly said. "What happened to knocking?"

Fran rocked on her heels, her hands hidden behind her back. She was already dressed in her school uniform. Milly could tell their dad had helped tie a purple ribbon in her hair — her ponytail was rather messy, and the ribbon was slightly wrinkled.

"Will you fix my hair?" Fran asked. "Dad tried today, but Mum's usually the one who does it…"

"Oh, sure," Milly said. "Come on, then."

Fran stood in front of the mirror while Milly carefully undid her ponytail. She began brushing out her hair, gently working through the knots with her fingers.

"Ouch," Fran said. "You're hurting me!"

"Oh, stop," Milly replied. "You're so dramatic… There." She finished tying the ribbon in Fran's hair and fluffed out her ponytail. "You know, you're probably old enough to do this on your own."

"Mum was teaching me how," Fran said quietly. "But… you know."

"Yeah. I know."

Milly glanced at her alarm clock, then at her pillow, where the strange white cloth was tucked underneath.

"It's almost time to go," she said. "Did Dad make breakfast?"

Fran shrugged. "There's cereal."

"Brilliant."

~

John Wilkes Secondary School was small and charming despite the building being old and somewhat rundown. The secondary school was also much closer to Milly's house compared to the primary school. She could easily walk there, which gave her dad more time to drive Charlie and Fran to Riverside Primary.

John Wilkes Secondary was sandwiched between a public park and a cemetery. Milly sometimes enjoyed feeding bits of bread to the ducks, swimming in the park's pond and exploring the cemetery with her friends. Lately, though, she hadn't had time for either — when she wasn't doing homework or practising netball, she was playing *War of the Ages 2* with Ashley and Lucy.

Milly met up with her friends at the front entrance, and together, they walked to their first class of the day: history. She was glad to have history first thing in the morning. It came naturally to her and was her favourite subject.

The history teacher, Mr Hayes, was fresh out of university. Milly enjoyed his lessons because, rather than simply reading from the textbook, he told stories. These stories mesmerised her, even though they were about people who had lived ages ago. Ashley liked history, too,

17

although she preferred maths, while Lucy was fairly indifferent. Harry, on the other hand, despised history and often copied off his best friend Chris's homework.

Milly settled at her desk behind Chris and next to Harry. A mischievous — but undeniably funny — idea for a prank popped into her head. She tapped Harry lightly on the shoulder, grinning as she batted her eyelashes at him.

"You ready for today's exam?"

"What?" Harry ran his fingers through his dark, gelled-back hair and let out an enormous sigh. "There's an exam today? Since when?"

"You didn't study?" Ashley asked as she sat down on Harry's other side. Catching on to Milly's joke, she played along. "Oh, Harry. You're in trouble."

Harry held his head in his hands. "Oh, man. My dad's gonna kill me if I fail another exam." He turned to look at the back of Chris's ginger head. "Hey, Chris, can I copy off you?"

"Huh?" Chris turned around to face him. "There's no exam today, Harry. They're messing with you."

"Oh," Harry said, looking mildly relieved. Then, realising he'd been duped, he glared at Milly. "Hey!"

"Only joking," Milly said, stifling a giggle.

The bell rang, signalling the start of class.

Mr Hayes walked into the small classroom, carrying a stack of papers in his arms. "Good morning, class," he said, his glasses slipping slightly down his nose. He plopped the papers onto his desk and stood in front of the chalkboard.

"Now, I know you've all read Chapter Three," he said, giving Harry a knowing look, "but let's do a bit of review, shall we?"

18

Milly got out her pen and notebook. History was one of the few classes where she actually took notes instead of spacing out and doodling in the margins.

A few hours later, Milly and her friends grabbed their lunches from the canteen and sat together at a picnic table in the courtyard to eat. Lunch was bangers and mash with a side of peas — Milly's favourite. She had also picked up a Red Bull from the vending machine, so she was all set.

Lucy looked at her lunch with disdain. "I really need to start packing my own lunches," she said, crinkling her nose. "This is foul."

"Oh, come off it," Ashley said. "It's not that bad."

After stuffing their faces for a few minutes, Milly took a sip of her energy drink and cleared her throat. She couldn't stop thinking about the white cloth with the golden thread she'd tucked under her pillow that morning. It looked exactly like how Mr Hayes had described Athena's Shawl during a lesson a few months ago.

Should I tell my friends about it? She thought. *Nah... they'll never believe me.*

Still, the situation was far too strange to keep to herself. She noticed a spider crawling towards her on the picnic table and moved her lunch tray slightly to the right. She didn't care for spiders.

"Um…" she began, trying her best to ignore it. "Do you guys remember that lecture Mr Hayes gave ages ago? About Athena's Shawl?"

"Mmm, yeah," Ashley said, swallowing a mouthful of mashed potatoes. "It was quite good, wasn't it?"

"What made you think of that?" Lucy asked.

"Just…" Milly stammered, glancing nervously at the spider as it crept closer. She didn't want to smash it with her tray, but she also didn't want it to crawl on her. Taking a breath, she tore her eyes away from it.

"Do you think Athena's Shawl could be real?"

"Are you thick?" Harry bit into a banger, its juices dripping onto the front of his uniform. He didn't seem to notice. "Mr Hayes was spouting a bunch of rubbish."

"It's mythology," Milly said, glaring at him. "Not rubbish."

"'It's mythology, not rubbish!'" Harry mimicked her in a high-pitched, fake-girly voice. "What's the difference?"

To Milly's horror, Harry scooped up the spider in his hands and placed it directly onto her lunch tray. She screamed and jumped up from the table as Harry burst out laughing.

"What's your problem? It's just a little spider."

Ashley glanced at Milly with an expression that clearly said: *This is the guy you fancy?*

Milly rolled her eyes and stuck her tongue out at Harry. Walking back to the table, she finished the rest of her Red Bull in one long gulp.

"Whatever," she said, refusing to give him the satisfaction of a reaction. "Are we playing *War of the Ages 2* later?"

"Of course," Lucy said. "What else would we do?"

"I can't," Chris said. "Too much homework."

"Nerd," Harry said, punching him playfully on the shoulder.

Chris rubbed his arm, a reluctant grin spreading across his face. "You're studying with me, aren't you, Harry? You said you wanted to pass your maths exam."

"Oh, right," Harry muttered, rubbing his eyes with a dramatic yawn. "Guess I can't play either," he said to Milly. "Apparently, I'm studying with Chris."

"I'll be there," Ashley said. "After netball practice."

"That's right, girl," Lucy said, beaming. "You brought your trainers, didn't you?" She pointed at Ashley's Ugg boots.

"Uh, no?" Ashley replied. "Is it really that big of a deal?"

"Guess you'll have to wait and see," Milly said, grinning as Lucy giggled.

The bell rang, signalling there were only ten minutes until their next class.

"See you guys at practice then, yeah?" Milly said.

They got up from the picnic table and made their way back to the canteen to stack their trays.

"See you then, Milly!" Ashley called.

~

When Milly got home that evening, still slightly sweating from netball practice, the house was unusually quiet. Louie was curled up asleep in his basket by the radiator in the hall. She kicked off her shoes, set her schoolbag down in the foyer, and shuffled in her socks to the kitchen to make herself a snack.

A note on the counter caught her eye: *Milly, I've gone grocery shopping. Charlie is at football practice, and Fran is at a friend's house. See you in an hour or so!*

Milly shrugged and started putting together a plate of cheese and crackers. Louie, the little scoundrel that he was, suddenly came bounding into the kitchen, barking his head off.

"What is it, Louie?" Milly asked, holding her plate of cheese and crackers away from him. "This is not for you. I'll get you some of your special Louie chewies from my room. You love those"

She headed up to her bedroom, the little dog at her heels.

"You're going to make me trip," she muttered.

Once in her room, Milly sat down at her desk and turned on her computer, leaving the door open for Louie, who had started whining at her bed for some reason.

"Why are you acting so weird?" she asked, feeling a little uneasy.

Curious, she bent down and checked under her bed, then lifted the mattress to look for bedbugs or anything else unusual, but there was nothing.

"Chill out, Louie, here have a Louie chewie" she said.

Louie, however, wasn't having it. He jumped up onto her bed and continued whining for a few minutes before finally settling down and resting his head on her pillow while tucking into his treat.

"There you go," Milly said with a sigh. "Now I can concentrate on my game."

She was eager to play a bit of *War of the Ages 2* before her friends joined her later.

Booting up the game, Milly quickly found herself irritated by the glare on her screen. The setting sun was shining directly through her bedroom window at just the right angle to make it impossible to see what was happening.

"Curse the sun," she muttered, standing up to figure out a way to block the light.

Her room didn't have curtains, so she was at a loss for a moment before inspiration struck.

"The cloth!" she said. "Perfect!"

She went over to her bed, scratched Louie behind the ear as he tucked into the tasty chewie, and pulled the white cloth out from under her pillow. Louie sniffed at the cloth, then let out a low growl—a behaviour Milly had only ever seen when he was playing tug-of-war.

"This isn't a toy, boy," she said. "I'm just going to use it to dull the sunlight a bit."

Louie huffed in apparent disapproval, and Milly grabbed a roll of tape from her desk drawer. Carefully, she used two pieces of tape to secure the cloth over her window. The sunlight still filtered through, but at least the annoying glare on her screen was gone.

"That's better," she said, sitting back down.

With the glare no longer an issue, Milly immersed herself in the world of *War of the Ages 2*.

Wolfstan, Mirabel, Faramund, and Captain Catalina were walking with King Jason III along a narrow trail in the forest, just outside the enemy stronghold. They passed by the mossy marble columns and ancient runes that they'd hidden behind just hours before. Then, the trail narrowed even more, and they had to walk single file, all the while being stared down by several rather off-putting statues.

A text bubble popped up next to the king:

My feet hurt.

"The ship is just around the bend, your Majesty," Wolfstan said, his own text bubble slightly overlapping with King Jason's.

"I can't believe we're going home," Faramund said, glancing wearily at the statues lining the trail.

"Yes," said the King. "And I cannot thank you enough for saving me."

Louie started barking again, and Milly wheeled around in her chair to see what he was on about. He yapped and growled at the cloth hung up in the window, which was catching the shadows of the scene playing out on Milly's computer screen.

"Huh," Milly said, a bit puzzled. "It's just from my game," she told Louie. "There's really no need to bark at everything, you know."

This only seemed to encourage Louie. He jumped up, his front feet pressed against the wall underneath the window, and began to tug at the corner of the cloth with his teeth.

"Louie," Milly said, her annoyance growing as she tried to move Louie away with her foot whilst just catching the cloth. "Stop that!"

Louie jumped at the cloth, and, bafflingly, disappeared into it. For a second, Milly thought he had jumped through the window, but the glass was still intact, and the cloth — now hanging in front of the window by one piece of tape — was still full of shadows.

Milly stared in confusion at it for a while, and then, as if realising what had happened, she flopped down to the floor in shock.

"What the…" She could feel her heart beating frantically in her chest, threatening to fall out onto the floor. She could clearly hear her blood thumping in her veins. "Louie! Oh my God!"

Gathering her thoughts, she rushed over to the cloth, calling for Louie, hoping, against all odds, that he could still hear her, somehow.

Shaking slightly, she reached out to touch the cloth with her fingertips. She expected to feel the windowpane behind the cloth, but to her surprise, her fingers went right through it. No… not through it, exactly. Into it. Just like Louie had. She gasped and backed away from the cloth. Despite knowing that her fingers were all still there, she counted them, then counted them again. They didn't feel any different. A bit tingly, maybe.

"What is this?" Milly said. "Oh, Louie. What am I going to do?"

Naturally, she felt inclined to wait until her dad got home from the store. That would be the responsible thing to do. She was worried about Louie, though. What would happen to him if she waited too long? And what was she supposed to tell her dad, anyway?

"Hey, Dad, Louie jumped into a cloth that I found while snooping around in Mum's closet, and now he's trapped in... in the cloth?"

No. He would never believe her. Besides, her curiosity was killing her. She had to know where Louie had gone. She took a deep breath and stuck her hand into the cloth, this time up to her elbow.

She leaned forward, and, moments later, found herself falling into an entirely different world.

Chapter 3
A Familiar Place

Milly opened her eyes. She felt like she'd just had the wind knocked out of her, and maybe she had — she was flat on her back, staring up at what appeared to be an overgrown forest canopy. Sunlight peeked through the leaves of the trees, creating playful patterns on the soft bed of moss where she found herself. A gust of wind whipped her hair into her face and made the trees groan in anguish, sending a shiver down her spine. Somehow, she had lost her hair tie.

"Ugh…" she said, rubbing the back of her head, which should have hurt, considering the fall she'd just had, but it didn't. "Where am I?" Milly hoisted herself up from the ground and took in the scene around her. It was like nothing she'd ever seen before — broken marble columns covered in moss that housed bugs and mushrooms. Enormous trees and a cerulean stream, rich with fish. She thought she could hear voices too — fearful cries for help and blades clashing nearby. A battle? She thought to herself. Was the white cloth a portal that had dropped her into the middle of… a war?

As Milly wandered through the woods, she stumbled upon ancient ruins partially concealed behind hollowed-out tree stumps and tangled vines. There was something… familiar about them. Where have I seen these before? she wondered. What exactly is going on here?

She began to follow a narrow path lined with enigmatic statues. They bore an uncanny resemblance to the ones from War of Ages 2, but Milly shook her head. No… that can't be right. It was difficult to be certain, anyway. War of Ages 2 was all pixels and sharp edges. These statues, however, felt tangible, almost alive. Their stoic expressions sent a shiver down her spine, but she forced herself to press on.

"I have to find Louie," she murmured to herself. "Maybe this path will lead to a village."

The forest seemed to be a mixture of the fantastical and the ancient, with creatures flitting about in the shadows and vines that waltzed to the music of the wind. The distant sounds of battle grew louder, and Milly quickened her pace, her heart pounding in her chest. War of Ages 2 was being projected onto the cloth when Louie and I fell into it, she thought to herself. Could I... could I really be inside my computer game? She shook her head, laughing a little. "There's no way," she said out loud. "This has got to be a dream."

Finally, Milly came upon a clearing. At the edge of the clearing was a quaint cottage built from mud and bricks. Milly's first thought was that the cottage was abandoned. After all, it looked rather ramshackle and rundown. Then, she could have sworn she saw someone in the window — a woman with dark hair that flowed past her shoulders. To her surprise, Milly didn't feel afraid. "Maybe she can help me," she said. "Maybe she's seen Louie." She approached the cottage and knocked tentatively on the thin, wooden door. She heard some muffled groans and a dog barking. Louie?

The dark-haired woman opened the door. Milly gasped upon seeing her up close — she was dressed in white robes and wore a blindfold over her eyes. Her lips were painted red, and when she turned to the side, Milly noticed an enormous pair of angel wings extending out from her back. "Why have you come here, child?" The woman spoke with a syrupy voice. "I do not smell evil or hubris on you... perhaps you're looking to seek vengeance on someone who has wronged you?"

Milly stared at her. "Uh... what? No, I'm just trying to find my —" Suddenly, Louie darted out from between the woman's legs and started jumping all over Milly. "Louie! You're okay!" She reached down to pick him up, and he licked her face. "What are you doing here, boy. Wait a sec I have some chewies in my pocket?"

"I found him wandering around in the forest," the strange woman said. "He seems happy to see you. Animals are great judges of character... therefore, you have my trust."

"O...kay," Milly said, holding Louie in her arms while handing him a Louie chewie and peering into the little cottage. "Um... do you think you can help me get home?" Just then, she noticed the people bound and gagged on the floor in the corner. "What the..." Somehow, she felt like she knew them. The one closest to her — a young man with black hair, tanned skin, and a bow and arrow strapped to his back — noticed Milly and gave a muffled shout.

"Help!"   "Wolfstan!" Milly said, finally putting two and two together. She slapped her palm against her forehead. "Oh my God. I'm in War of the Ages 2." She turned to the woman, putting her hands on her hips. "Okay, so, I know I'm in a dream right now, but I might as well play along," she said. "Why do you have the War of the Ages characters tied up in your house?"

"War of the Ages..." the woman said. "Yes, there is a war. But why do you speak such nonsense, my child? These people have done something quite evil, and it is my job to restore balance to the world by punishing them."

Wolfstan, Mirabel, Faramund, and King Jason struggled and writhed on the floor. Catalina furrowed her eyebrows and stuck her tongue out like she was concentrating on something. A moment later, a grin flashed across her face. "Got it!" She said, spitting out her gag, and breaking free from the cloth tied around her wrists. She hoisted herself up off the floor and pointed a small dagger at the blindfolded woman. "Nemesis! Free us now! We've done nothing wrong!"

The woman — Nemesis — didn't flinch. She smiled. "Even if I choose to let you go, fate will have its way with you eventually," she said. "That's the way of the world."

Captain Catalina, sensing that Nemesis wasn't going to do anything, took the opportunity to undo the restraints of her comrades. "She's the goddess of vengeance," she said to Milly. "You can't trust her."

Wolfstan, Mirabel, Faramund, and the King sat up, taking out their gags and rubbing their wrists. "Thank you, Catalina," Faramund said. "I'm honestly not sure what we would do without you." Wolfstan — who was never one to let his guard down in War of Ages 2 — drew his bow, pointing it at Nemesis.

"Hey, Wolfstan," Mirabel said, nudging him with her elbow. "Not in front of the kid."

Wolfstan glanced at Milly and lowered his bow. Milly just stood there, holding Louie in her arms and thinking to herself: This might be the best dream I've ever had. She couldn't contain herself any longer. "This is so cool!" She said, grinning from ear to ear. "I love you guys! I play your game all the time!"

Mirabel gave her a sceptical look. "What game?"

"War of the Ages 2," Milly said. "It's my favourite computer game."

"What's a computer?" Wolfstan said. "I don't trust you, little girl." He gave her a quick once-over. "What are you wearing? I've never seen garbs like that."

Milly remembered that she was still wearing her netball uniform and felt a little embarrassed. She did not doubt in her mind that she stuck out like a sore thumb — but whatever. This was a dream. Right? "Uh…

it's my netball uniform," she said, trying to ignore Nemesis's cold laugh. "I'm… from a different place and time."

"Where?" Wolfstan asked. "When?"

"Eastbourne, England," Milly told him. "In the 21st century."

Faramund gave her a blank look and whispered something in Catalina's ear. Catalina nodded, then turned to Milly. "How did you get here, then?" The way she said it, Milly could tell that she didn't believe her.

"I…" Milly found herself stumbling over her words. "My dog jumped into a white cloth that I found in my Mum's closet. And then, I sort of… followed him in."

"A white cloth?" King Jason spoke up. "Did it have golden threads sewn into it?"

"Yeah…" Milly said. "How do you know that?"

The War of the Ages 2 characters gave each other pointed looks. Catalina nodded her head at the king. Meanwhile, Nemesis was rummaging around in a large chest near her bed. She pulled out a long sword and started for the front door. "I need to sharpen my sword," she said. "Come outside when you're ready to face me. I'd rather not bloody up my house." She closed the door behind her, and Louie barked.

"Stay here," Catalina said, going up to Milly and putting her arm around her. "We want to talk to you, but we have to fight Nemesis, first."

Faramund materialised on the other side of Milly. "Stick with us, kid," he said. "We'll help you and your dog get home."

"O…okay," Milly felt a bit uncomfortable. She hadn't gotten to the point in War of the Ages 2 yet where the warriors face off against Nemesis. Still, though, she trusted them to protect her. These were the characters that she and her friends always played as, after all! She knew them better than anyone. "Is there anything I can do to help?"

Wolfstan drew his bow once more. "Stay out of our way," he said. "We're heroes, you know."

"I know," she said, scratching Louie behind his ear. "Okay. We'll wait here."

The knights and King Jason rushed outside, led by Captain Catalina. Milly's eyes widened like saucers as she peered through the open window. The forest surrounding the clearing whispered with an eerie stillness, broken only by the rustling of leaves stirred by a sudden gust of wind. In the heart of the clearing stood five figures, their faces grim and determined in the dappled moonlight.

Captain Catalina twirled twin knives with expert precision, her gaze fixed on Nemesis. King Jason, a crown of leaves adorning his golden hair, wielded a bejewelled sword, its blade shimmering like liquid silver. Hidden in the shadows, Wolfstan nocked an arrow to his bow. Meanwhile, Mirabel and Faramund stood side by side, their swords raised in perfect unison. Nemesis, still wearing her blindfold, grinned as she held up her own sword.

The first clash shattered the silence as Wolfstan released an arrow, the projectile streaking towards Nemesis with deadly precision. The goddess sidestepped with ease, the arrow hissing past her, disturbing only the still air. King Jason lunged forward, his sword slicing through the shadows, but Nemesis danced out of reach, her retaliatory strike sending the king sprawling to the ground.

Undeterred, Captain Catalina leapt into action, her knives flashing as she wove through Nemesis's attacks with graceful precision. Each strike was calculated, her movements fluid and fierce. Mirabel and Faramund joined the fray, their swords clashing against the goddess's blade in a furious symphony of steel.

31

Milly's heart pounded as she watched the battle unfold. Wolfstan continued firing arrows from the shadows, his aim unyielding. Catalina, with unmatched agility, dodged and parried Nemesis's relentless strikes, her twin blades a whirlwind of deadly elegance. Mirabel and Faramund moved as one, their synchronised attacks creating a formidable defence against the goddess's onslaught.

As the skirmish raged, the sun dipped below the horizon, and the forest was bathed in moonlight. The clearing, now stained with blood, grew eerily quiet. Suddenly, an anguished cry pierced the stillness as one of Wolfstan's arrows found its mark. Mirabel surged forward, her sword cutting through the darkness.

And then it happened — a foreboding hush fell over the clearing as Nemesis crumbled into nothingness.

Faramund, Mirabel, and Wolfstan exchanged words of triumph as Catalina helped King Jason to his feet. Though they had claimed victory, Milly couldn't shake the gnawing feeling that the true battle had only just begun.

Chapter 4
The Priest

That night, they ate Nemesis's food and made themselves comfortable in her home. It felt wrong somehow, even though Nemesis had tried to kill them. Milly couldn't quite stomach the bread, cheese, and fruit, despite it being unbelievably delicious. She hadn't wanted anyone to die—not for real. She was also beginning to suspect that this wasn't a dream, which made her feel like she might cry, throw up, or both.

The warriors, however, were joyous and drunk on their victory and the goddess's wine.

"Wait until my wife hears that I took down a goddess!" Wolfstan boasted.

"Well, technically, I'm the one who delivered the final blow," Mirabel said, sipping her wine from a large wooden cup. "But it was a group effort."

"She'll be back," Faramund said. "You can't really kill a goddess."

"Yeah, but it could take ages for her to regenerate," Wolfstan replied, waving away Faramund's concern. "We'll be long gone by then."

King Jason hadn't said much all night. He drank his wine and stared at Milly.

"So," he said during a lull in the conversation, "you have the Shawl of Athena."

Milly gave him a blank look. "The Shawl of Athena?"

Catalina polished off her piece of bread. "The Shawl of Athena," she repeated. "Otherwise known as Athena's Shawl. Have you heard of it?"

"Um... my history teacher gave a lesson about it recently," Milly said. "But he said it was just a myth."

"Where is it?" King Jason asked. Something in his eyes unsettled Milly. "Can I see it?"

"I don't have it with me," she told him. "It's at my parents' house."

The king smiled beneath his thick moustache. He rubbed his hands together like a housefly delighted to find a rotting apple core.

"And where is your parents' house?"

"Mmm," Faramund said, swallowing a mouthful of cheese and washing it down with a sip of wine. "England, remember? 21st century."

"Oh, right," King Jason muttered. He pursed his lips, rubbing his temples with his fingers. He sighed heavily and ran a hand through his hair. It reminded Milly of how Harry acted when he was frustrated.

"So... what's the big deal with Athena's Shawl?" she asked. "I found it in my mother's closet."

"Athena's Shawl disappeared a long time ago," Catalina explained. "King Jason has been searching for it for decades."

"Right... my history teacher mentioned that," Milly said, eyeing the king warily. "Why are you looking for it?"

"Athena's Shawl holds unimaginable power," Wolfstan said, leaning back in his chair. "I can't believe a little girl ended up with it."

"I'm not a little girl," Milly protested. "I just turned twelve!"

"Yeah... you're a little girl," Faramund said. "Why do you have Athena's Shawl? Did you steal it?"

"How would she have done that?" Mirabel chimed in. "She's just a kid."

"Well, apparently, she can travel through time and space."

"Right... because of Athena's Shawl. Probably."

Faramund rolled his eyes at Mirabel, then turned to the king. "We're not going to get to go home for a while yet, are we?"

King Jason arched an eyebrow. "Not if there's a chance we could find Athena's Shawl," he said, looking intently at Milly. "Little girl, I command you to take us back to your time and hand over the shawl immediately."

"My name is Milly," she said through gritted teeth. "Well, actually, it's Amelia, but everyone calls me Milly. And I don't know how to get home. That's what you're supposed to help me with!" She instinctively glanced down at Louie and added, "And get Louie back, too."

"You came here without a plan to get back?" Wolfstan asked, raising an eyebrow. "Huh."

"I was just trying to save my dog," Milly said, her gaze dropping to Louie, who was happily sleeping under the table. "But, yeah... now I don't know how to get back home."

Everyone at the table went quiet for a few moments. Faramund picked his teeth with his fingers, while Catalina stared up at the ceiling.

"What?" Milly said, breaking the silence, unable to bear it any longer.

"I'm just thinking," Catalina said. "See, we're from England too—and France, as well. We don't really know anyone here."

35

"Yeah, and the villagers probably hate us because we raided their fortress," Faramund added. "Whatever! We were just trying to get our king back. It's not like we raided their temple. That was the Persians."

Wolfstan poured himself another cup of wine and began peeling a fresh pomegranate. "They didn't find what they were looking for, though," he said. "Rumour has it a corrupt priest—one of their own—stole Athena's Shawl."

"Yep," Faramund said, nodding. "And no one's seen the priest since."

He pushed his chair back, stood up, and flopped onto the goddess's bed. "I don't know about you lot, but I'm exhausted. We can look for King Jason's stupid shawl in the morning, yeah?" He pulled the blankets over his head and, within minutes, began snoring.

"Ignore Faramund," Catalina said, rolling her eyes. "He's just annoyed because he wants to go home."

"We all want to go home," Wolfstan muttered.

"You have a duty to serve the kingdom," King Jason snapped. "I don't want to hear any more complaining. And shouldn't I be the one who gets the bed? I *am* the king, after all!"

Mirabel shot Milly a sheepish smile, as though apologising for the behaviour of her king and companions. She must have noticed Milly's growing anxiety because she leaned over and patted her shoulder.

"Don't worry," Mirabel said. "We'll make sure you get home. Whatever it takes."

~

The next day, they set off down the same trail they had come from, the morning sun warming their bodies. The statues seemed a little less intimidating with the warriors around. For the first time since Milly had found herself in this strange world, she felt a flicker of hope.

"So, I came up with a plan while you lot were sleeping," Catalina announced, leading the way as usual. "We disguise ourselves as villagers, talk to some locals, and see what they know."

The group was oddly quiet behind her. Catalina stopped and turned around to face them. "What? It's a good place to start."

"I suppose so," Wolfstan said, scratching his beard. "How are we going to get disguises?"

Catalina came to an abrupt halt in the middle of the trail.

"What is it?" Faramund asked, trying his best to avoid bumping into the king, who was walking just ahead of him.

"See for yourself," Catalina said, a smile spreading across her face.

A few hundred yards ahead, what appeared to be a family — dressed in beige robes and leather sandals — sat around a campfire. The scent of something honey-infused wafted through the air, and they seemed to be eating stew.

Milly squinted to get a better look. There was a mother, a father, and three teenagers. Her gaze darted between the warriors and the family, then back to Catalina. She raised an eyebrow. "You want to knock them out and steal their clothes? There are only five people, and we need six."

Catalina's grin widened, her eyes sparkling with excitement. "They won't get hurt, and we can find another robe somewhere. But yes, that's one way to put it. We'll approach them and have a friendly chat. While we're doing that, Wolfstan will take them out one by one with his sleep arrows."

"You have sleep arrows?" Milly folded her arms. "Since when?" She hadn't gotten very far in *War of the Ages 2*, so maybe she'd missed Wolfstan upgrading his bow.

Wolfstan patted his quiver proudly. "Finally. I've been waiting for a chance to use these."

Milly exchanged uneasy glances with the rest of the group.

King Jason let out a dramatic sigh. "I never thought I'd stoop to stealing clothes from peasants to blend in."

"Ha!" Faramund pumped his fist in the air. "That'll be a sight to see. I'm in."

The group cautiously approached the campfire. As they drew closer, Milly felt a pang of guilt. The family was deep in conversation, oblivious to what was about to happen.

"Hello there!" Catalina called out, flashing a warm smile. "We got lost in the woods and were hoping for some guidance. Mind if we join you by the fire?"

The family looked up, confusion plain on their faces. After a moment, the father — whom Milly assumed was the head of the family — gestured for them to sit.

Milly, King Jason, and the warriors settled around the fire, engaging in polite conversation while Catalina subtly signalled to Wolfstan, who was hiding in the tall grass nearby.

Wolfstan acted quickly. One by one, he shot the villagers in the arm with his sleep arrows, and they slumped into a deep slumber.

The king took the father's clothes, while Mirabel, the tallest warrior, took the mother's robe. "Sorry," she murmured, draping her own cloak over the sleeping woman for modesty. "Milly, the daughter looks about your size."

Faramund, Wolfstan, and Milly hastily swapped clothes with the three teenagers. It was an awkward process for Milly, and guilt gnawed at her as she removed the girl's robe. Interrupting the family's breakfast and taking their clothes felt wrong, but she reminded herself that getting home was the priority.

Catalina rummaged through the family's belongings and triumphantly held up a spare robe. "I've found something!" she declared.

Meanwhile, Louie sniffed at the father's unfinished stew. He looked up at Milly, tilting his head curiously.

She laughed despite herself. "Go on, Louie, I've run out of Louie chewies" she said.

Louie eagerly dipped his head into the bowl and began devouring the stew, his tail wagging happily.

"Switch with me, Faramund," Wolfstan grumbled, tugging at the too-tight robes. The ill-fitting outfit left his legs exposed and made him look like a bulging sack of flour. "This scrawny boy's clothes are cutting off my circulation."

"No way," Faramund said, laughing. "It's not my fault you devoured an entire loaf of bread last night."

Their bickering carried on until Captain Catalina intervened. "Faramund, switch with Wolfstan," she snapped. "He's our archer, and he needs to be able to move."

"Fine," Faramund muttered, rolling his eyes as he begrudgingly swapped clothes.

The group continued down the trail, heading towards the village. The chaos of the previous night seemed to have subsided, and the forest around them thinned as they walked. Louie's ears perked up as a distant dog barked.

"We're almost there," Catalina said. "Everyone act natural. We need to gain their trust and blend in."

Milly grew nervous as they approached the outskirts of the village. She scooped up Louie, holding his collar tightly. "We're going to need to find you a leash, boy," she said. "Can't have you running off again."

Walking beside Mirabel, Milly felt the need to confide in her. "You know," she said, her voice low, "my mum is missing. Do you think she fell into Athena's Shawl like I did?"

Mirabel shrugged. "It's possible, but no one really understands how Athena's Shawl works."

Milly frowned, her mind racing. She remembered how her mum had once had possession of the Shawl—a fact that both puzzled and gave her hope. *Mum has to be nearby,* she thought. *She just has to be.* Her grip on Louie's collar slackened as she let her thoughts wander.

Before she could react, Louie wriggled free and bolted towards the village.

"Louie Roi! Get back here!" Milly shouted, dashing after him.

"Don't make a scene!" Catalina called out, exasperated, as the group hurried after Milly.

Milly sprinted through the cobblestone streets, her stolen sandals slapping loudly. Louie made a beeline for a meat stand in the bustling market, where vendors sold colourful fabrics, gleaming trinkets, and mouth-watering food.

As she chased Louie, Milly accidentally knocked over a barrel of live fish. The slippery creatures flopped desperately on the ground, drawing disapproving looks from villagers.

"Sorry! Sorry!" Milly stammered, trying to scoop up the fish. But her efforts only caused more chaos as jewellery stands were jostled, fruit baskets overturned, and tempers flared.

A middle-aged woman with a woven basket approached, her sharp eyes scanning Milly. "I haven't seen you before," she said. "Who are you, and what business do you have here?"

Catalina stepped in, her tone calm but authoritative. "Apologies for the commotion. We're travellers seeking shelter and provisions. Our village was attacked, and we barely escaped with our lives."

The woman's eyes narrowed. "And you expect us to believe that? Our village has its own troubles. We can't afford to harbour strangers."

Milly took a deep breath and spoke up. "Please, we're just passing through. My mother is missing, and we're trying to find her. We won't trouble your village, I promise."

At that moment, Louie trotted back to her, his tail between his legs and a stolen piece of meat dangling from his mouth.

"Your mother is missing?" The woman's face softened slightly. As she watched Milly and the others gather the fallen fruit, her tone became less guarded. "What does she look like? Perhaps someone here has seen her."

Wolfstan, Faramund, and King Jason finally caught up. The king collapsed onto the cobblestones, panting and sweating under his disguise. Faramund and Wolfstan began fanning him with their hands as the midday heat bore down.

Milly knelt to pick up some of the fruit. "Um…" Milly felt her heart pounding in her chest. "She has long blonde hair, blue eyes, and would have been dressed in posh clothes and Tiffany jewellery." She hesitated, realising the woman probably wouldn't recognise such references. "Well… never mind about the clothes. She looks a bit like me and would have stood out like a sore thumb." She paused, uncertain whether to explain she was from a different time. She'd have to tell someone eventually — wasn't that the point of coming to the village?

Her voice steady despite her nerves. "She might have been carrying a strange piece of cloth—something like a shawl."

The woman nodded thoughtfully, her gaze shifting between Milly and her companions. "Stay here," she said. "I'll see what I can find out."

As the woman disappeared into the crowd, Milly looked down at Louie, who had already finished the stolen meat. "You're going to get us in so much trouble," she muttered, scratching his ears. Despite everything, she couldn't help but smile.

Mirabel and Catalina finished gathering the woman's scattered fruit, placing it back in the basket. "Thank you," the woman said, balancing the basket expertly on her head. "I haven't seen anyone like that around here," she said to Milly, "but I know someone who might be able to help. He's the one who makes the rules around here. If anyone saw something — like an abduction — they'd report it to him."

"Can you take us to him?" Milly asked, trying to keep her eagerness in check. "Please?"

The woman nodded slowly. "I suppose so. But you'll need to keep that dog of yours under control. The priest doesn't care much for dogs."

"Oh, thank you!" Milly said, trailing after her. "I'll find a rope or something to tie onto his collar."

"Milly, hold on," Mirabel said, grabbing her wrist. "We need to be careful, okay? We don't know who we can trust."

"This lady seems nice," Milly replied. "Come on! Let's go talk to this priest. Maybe he can help me get home."

42

"Mirabel is right," Catalina interjected, helping King Jason to his feet. "But… we don't have many options. Let's see what this priest has to say, but stay alert."

"Do computer game characters automatically think everything is some sort of trap?" Milly asked with a hint of sarcasm.

"We're not computer game characters," Wolfstan muttered. "I really wish you'd stop saying that."

Milly ignored him, scanning the area for a rope as they followed the woman through the residential part of the village. Small homes lined the dusty streets, their walls weathered and roofs patched with straw. "I mean, it's not like she's leading us to the priest who stole Athena's Shawl, right? He's literally stuck in Athena's Shawl."

The group fell silent. Milly glanced over her shoulder. "Right?"

Mirabel hesitated. "Well, he *is* stuck in Athena's Shawl… but no one really knows what that means." She exchanged a wary look with Catalina. "You're stuck in Athena's Shawl, too, aren't you? For all we know, the priest who stole the Shawl could be here somewhere."

"Yeah… or maybe not," Faramund added. "That's why everyone wants to get their hands on it. It works in mysterious ways."

"Okay, well, I'll never get home if we're too afraid to try anything," Milly said. She spotted a frayed piece of rope next to a wooden bucket filled with rust-coloured water. Bending down, she picked it up and tied it to Louie's collar. "Also, Athena's Shawl is at my house for some reason, so I'm guessing you lot will want to come home with me."

She smiled to herself at the thought of the War of the Ages 2 characters wandering around Eastbourne, England. It would be a sight. Most people would probably think they were cosplayers, so they wouldn't stand out… too much.

"That's right," King Jason said firmly. "We need to bring the child home and take possession of Athena's Shawl. No matter what it takes."

"I'd love to see England again. Well… future England, that is," Faramund said, stretching his arms over his head with a grin. "Are there loads of good-looking women there?"

"As if they'd fancy you, Faramund," Wolfstan quipped with an impish grin. Faramund responded with a playful punch to his shoulder. "Ow…"

Milly, meanwhile, found herself lost in thought. She couldn't stop worrying about her friends, her dad, and her siblings back home. Were they worried sick about her? She whispered a quick prayer in her head: *Please, oh please, let me get home soon.* Still, the thought of her mother possibly being here kept her grounded. She was determined to find her first.

They followed the kind woman, her fruit basket bobbing slightly above the heads of the crowd. She led them out of the residential area and onto a dirt path riddled with tree roots. As they walked, the mud-brick buildings gave way to groves of gnarled olive trees. Milly slipped slightly on a mossy patch but managed to steady herself. A knot tightened in her stomach, and Louie began whining incessantly, as though sensing something was off.

The group fell silent, their unease palpable. Even Faramund and Wolfstan had stopped joking. Milly couldn't shake the tension in the air. Everyone was wondering the same thing: where exactly was this woman taking them?

"Where are we going?" King Jason finally asked, his tone sharp with impatience. "Are we there yet?"

"Almost," the woman replied calmly. "Be patient and remain silent as you were before. The temple is a sacred place."

"So… about the priest that stole Athena's Shawl," Milly whispered to Mirabel, unable to shake her curiosity. "What did he look like? You know… just in case we run into him."

"Oh," Mirabel said, her voice low. "I've never seen him myself. I only know the story we told you earlier. But there are so many variations — it happened so long ago that no one's really sure what's true."

"Do you know his name?"

"Keep your voice down!" Catalina hissed, glancing at the woman ahead. She leaned closer to Milly. "Deimos Asgard," she whispered. "But no one's seen him in ages, remember? You've got nothing to worry about."

Just then, the woman came to an abrupt stop. Adjusting her basket of fruit, she pointed ahead. "The temple is just up that path," she said. "You'll find Father Alexiou there. He should be able to answer any questions you have."

Milly, feeling a little off-balance, offered her thanks. "Th-thank you. We're very grateful."

The woman nodded but seemed nervous. To Milly's surprise, she handed her the basket of fruit. "Would you mind giving this to Father Alexiou for me? I'd do it myself, but I'm terribly busy. Just… don't tell him the fruit fell on the ground, alright?"

"Uh… okay," Milly said, wrapping the frayed rope that served as Louie's leash around her wrist while balancing the basket in her arms. "Where exactly will we find him?"

"He's usually in the *naos*, praying to Athena. Just explain your business to the guards at the entrance and make your way to the centre of the temple."

"Thanks again," Catalina said, stepping forward to lead. "Is there any way we can repay you?"

The woman shook her head quickly. "Just deliver the basket to Father Alexiou. I have other matters to attend to." Without another word, she scurried off into the woods, leaving the group standing by the path.

"Okay…" Catalina said with a shrug. "Let's go, then."

They followed the path until it opened onto a long, stone staircase. At the top, Milly could see the ancient temple, and she gasped audibly. "Wow," she whispered. "It's beautiful, isn't it?"

The temple's architecture stirred memories of her history lessons with Mr. Hayes. Its symmetrical design featured a front porch supported by columns leading to the inner sanctuary—the *naos*, as the woman had called it. The sight felt both surreal and awe-inspiring.

As they ascended the stairs, Milly noticed two guards stationed at the temple entrance, their spears gleaming in the sunlight. She took a deep breath and stepped forward, but Captain Catalina stopped her with an outstretched arm.

"Wait," Catalina said. "Let me handle this."

Milly reluctantly stepped back, watching as Catalina addressed the guards with confidence. "We seek an audience with Father Alexiou," she said. "We have urgent matters to discuss."

The guards exchanged unreadable glances from behind their helmets. Finally, the one on the left spoke. "Urgent matters regarding what? Father Alexiou is very busy. He doesn't often meet with peasants."

"Peasants?" King Jason exclaimed, his indignation clear.

Catalina silenced him with a sharp look. "We bring information we believe he'll find important," she said smoothly.

"And this," Milly added, lifting the fruit basket.

The guards regarded the basket, then each other, before the one on the right nodded. "Very well. You may enter. Leave your weapons outside, and remember to conduct yourselves with respect."

Catalina gave a short bow. "Thank you, sirs."

Inside, the temple was cool and shadowy, with beams of sunlight streaming through narrow openings in the ceiling. The air was heavy with the scent of incense and age. Ahead, in the *naos*, Father Alexiou knelt in prayer before a weathered statue of Athena.

Catalina took the fruit basket from Milly and approached him cautiously. "Father Alexiou," she began, her voice steady, "we were told you could help us. We have some questions about Athena's Shawl."

The priest turned slowly, his deep-set eyes fixed on the group. His face, framed by bushy eyebrows and deep wrinkles, was inscrutable. "Athena's Shawl?" he repeated, his gaze lingering on Milly. Something about his expression made her uneasy.

He glanced at the basket. "Is that fruit for me?"

"Yes," Catalina said, placing it at his feet. "But it's not just fruit we bring. This girl"—she gestured toward Milly—"is from another time. The future. She says Athena's Shawl appeared in her home, and we're struggling to find a way to return her to her own time. We hoped you could shed some light on how the Shawl works."

Father Alexiou sighed heavily and plucked an apple from the basket. He took a deliberate bite before speaking. "The theft of Athena's Shawl is a story as old as time. Its secrets are complex, and its resolution has evaded even the wisest among us."

47

Milly stepped forward, unable to suppress her curiosity. "Have you ever encountered the priest who stole the Shawl? Do you know anything about him?"

The priest's expression darkened. His eyes narrowed, and his voice dropped to a gravelly tone. "I have heard whispers—fragments of a tale buried in the sands of time. If this priest ever lived, his existence is cloaked in mystery. But heed my warning: the threads of fate are fragile. To unravel them is to risk unintended consequences."

Faramund crossed his arms, his impatience breaking through. "No offence, but you look old enough to remember Methuselah. Surely you know something about where Deimos Asgard went—"

"We do not speak that name here!" Father Alexiou bellowed, his sudden anger reverberating through the temple.

Everyone froze, startled. Catalina recovered first, meeting his fierce gaze without flinching.

"He has been banished from the temple," Father Alexiou continued, his voice trembling with emotion. "This is a place of peace and worship. We must not disturb the goddess Athena."

"Understood," Catalina said carefully. Even Faramund looked uneasy, his earlier bravado fading.

Father Alexiou glared at the group for a moment longer before exhaling sharply. "If you seek answers, tread with care. The Shawl is no ordinary relic, and its power is not to be trifled with."

Catalina nodded. "Thank you, Father. Is there anything—anything at all—you can tell us that might help?"

Father Alexiou scratched his beard and chuckled softly. "You are fools for coming here without Athena's Shawl," he said, his gaze fixed on Milly. "Little girl, without the Shawl, there's no way for you to return home."

Milly's heart sank, and she swallowed hard. "But… how was I supposed to bring it? My dog fell into it, and then I followed him—"

"Your dog *fell into it*?" Father Alexiou interrupted, bursting into a deep, boisterous laugh. "That's absurd! I've never heard of such a thing. How could a dog activate Athena's Shawl?"

"Wait," King Jason interjected, his voice calm but commanding. He turned to Milly. "Tell us exactly what happened before you and your dog fell into Athena's Shawl."

Milly sighed, her cheeks flushing. "Well… I was in my room, playing my favourite game, *War of the Ages 2*. The sun was shining directly into my bedroom, so I decided to hang up the cloth—Athena's Shawl, I guess—in the window to block the glare." She hesitated, then continued. "My dog, Louie, started tugging on the corner of the Shawl. I noticed the shadows from my game moving on the cloth. And then…" She swallowed again, recalling the strange sensation. "Louie disappeared into it, and when I tried to grab him, I fell through too."

The group fell silent, exchanging puzzled looks.

"That's… quite the tale," Wolfstan said, scratching his head. "But we're not characters in some game. We're real people." He glanced at the others for affirmation. "Right?"

Faramund shrugged. "At this point, who even knows?"

"If we're characters in a computer game," Mirabel added, crossing her arms, "whatever a computer is… then…"

"Then nothing matters," Wolfstan finished, slumping against the temple wall and sliding to the floor. "I'm not real. My wife isn't real…" His voice trailed off.

"Don't think like that!" Milly exclaimed, her voice firm. "You're my heroes, all of you. Just because there's a version of you in my game doesn't mean you're not real. For all we know, the characters in *War of the Ages 2* could have been based on you."

Wolfstan glanced up, his brow furrowed. "Based on us?"

Milly nodded. "Maybe the creators of the game somehow knew about this world and used it as inspiration."

"And who created this game?" Catalina asked.

"Um… a big company," Milly said, wringing her hands. "I don't know the names of the people who worked on it. Probably a whole team."

"Very helpful," Faramund said with a roll of his eyes.

Meanwhile, Father Alexiou had stepped closer to King Jason, studying him intently. "You… look familiar," the priest said, his brow furrowed. "Have we met before?"

"I… I don't think so," King Jason replied, his voice wary.

Milly's heart raced. She remembered that King Jason had been a prisoner of Father Alexiou's people not long ago. She held her breath, praying the priest wouldn't recognise him.

"Why are you so interested in Athena's Shawl?" Father Alexiou asked suddenly, his tone sharp. "It doesn't belong to you." He turned away, folding his hands into the sleeves of his robes. "In fact, it doesn't belong to any of you."

"Then why did I find it in my mum's closet?" Milly countered.

Father Alexiou paused, stroking his beard thoughtfully. "A good question," he murmured. "I've spent years searching for Athena's Shawl. I always believed only the goddess herself knew where it had gone." His gaze drifted to the statue at the centre of the room. "But for reasons I cannot fathom, she has not answered my prayers."

"Maybe she doesn't want anyone to find it," Faramund said. "It *is* her Shawl, after all. Maybe she sent it to Milly's house to keep it safe from meddling hands."

"Maybe…" Catalina said, her voice tinged with doubt. "But why Milly's house? Could she be destined to protect the Shawl?"

Milly laughed nervously. "Look, I'm only twelve," she said. "Trusting me with something that important sounds like a really bad idea."

The group's discussion grew heated, voices overlapping as they debated what to do next. No one was paying attention to Louie, who had slipped free of his leash and was now exploring the small room.

Milly glanced at him briefly but, caught up in the argument, didn't think much of it. It wasn't until Louie began sniffing at the hem of Father Alexiou's robes that anyone noticed.

"Get off me!" Father Alexiou snapped, yanking the fabric away from the dog. "Stupid mutt!"

Louie whimpered but didn't retreat. Instead, he sniffed again, his nose pressing insistently against the priest's robes. Then, with a low growl, he bared his teeth. The growl escalated into sharp barks, echoing through the temple.

"Control your animal!" Father Alexiou roared, his face reddening. "What does it want from me? Go on — get away!"

Milly's heart raced as she watched Louie grow more agitated. She hated the way Father Alexiou had called him "stupid" and feared he might lash out at her beloved pet. "What's wrong, boy?" she asked, stepping forward to grab his leash.

Before she could reach him, Louie clamped his teeth onto the edge of Father Alexiou's robes and began tugging with surprising force.

"Louie Roi!" Milly called, her cheeks burning with embarrassment as she used his full name. He'd been named after King Louie from one of her favourite films, but right now, he wasn't acting very regal. "Let go! What are you doing?"

But Louie ignored her, his barking relentless as he pulled at the fabric. Milly had never seen him act this way before, and a troubling thought crept into her mind: maybe Father Alexiou wasn't as trustworthy as he seemed.

As the priest struggled to free himself, a small necklace tumbled from the folds of his robes and landed on the floor with a soft clink.

Milly's eyes widened in shock. The delicate chain and blue pendant were unmistakable. "That's my mum's necklace!" she blurted out, her voice trembling.

Father Alexiou froze, his expression shifting from anger to something more complex — a mix of surprise, guilt, and perhaps a touch of fear.

Milly stepped forward, her heart pounding. "Why do you have my mother's necklace, Father Alexiou?"

Chapter 5
The Portal

Milly quickly picked up the necklace from the floor and turned it over in her hands, examining the pendant and running her fingers along the silver chain. She looked at Father Alexiou, who was stumbling over his words, no doubt trying to come up with an excuse, and felt an overwhelming urge to punch him. Instead, she clutched the necklace tightly and felt hot, angry tears streaming down her cheeks.

"Where is my mother?" she demanded. "Where are you keeping her?"

"That… that's not your mother's necklace," Father Alexiou stammered, wringing his hands. His lip quivered, but Milly caught a glimmer of something sinister in his eyes—a barely concealed smile. "I merely found it lying on the ground the other day. I was planning to sell it to a merchant in the village."

"Liar!" Milly shouted. "You knew my mother had Athena's Shawl. You kidnapped her, hoping to steal it for yourself! But it didn't work, did it?"

"Milly," Mirabel interjected, stepping closer. "Calm down. We don't know for certain that Father Alexiou stole your mother's necklace."

"Why else would he have it?" Milly retorted, her heart pounding in her chest. "Mirabel, are you seriously buying this 'I found it on the ground' nonsense? I thought you were smarter than that!"

Mirabel's lips pressed into a thin line. She looked hurt, and Milly immediately regretted her words.

"I'm sorry," Milly said, wiping fresh tears from her eyes. "My mum has been missing for months. I'm so worried about her."

By now, Louie had let go of the priest's robes and was attempting to calm Milly, rubbing his back against her legs and pawing at her.

Behind them, Wolfstan reached for his bow but found it missing. He had been forced to leave it at the temple's entrance. Catalina caught his eye and gave the slightest shake of her head. Her expression seemed to say, *the time will come.*

Suddenly, a dilapidated section of the wall next to Milly and Louie began to warp and swirl. Milly gasped and pulled Louie back as a shimmering portal appeared.

"What on earth—" she began, but her words were cut off as two figures tumbled through the swirling wall and landed on the temple floor with a thud.

"Ouch…" Fran muttered, hauling herself up and brushing off her skirt. She was holding a framed picture of their parents, smiling in front of their house. A piece of Athena's Shawl peeked out from her shirt pocket.

"Fran?" Milly stared in disbelief.

"What is this place?" Charlie asked, his eyes wide as he took in their surroundings. "Hi, Milly!"

"Uh… hi, Charlie," Milly replied. "What are you two doing here? How did you get here?"

"What is going on?" Wolfstan demanded, looking increasingly paranoid. "Why are children coming out of the walls?"

"We came to find you," Fran explained. "When we got home and realised you and Louie weren't there, we went up to your room and saw your computer game was open."

"Yeah, and there was this weird white cloth hanging in the window," Charlie added. "At first, we didn't know what to do, but then—"

"Then we saw these characters on your computer screen who looked just like you and Louie," Fran interrupted, her excitement spilling over. "Your game was being projected onto the white cloth, probably because of the sunlight. So we went up to it, and—"

"We put our thinking caps on!" Charlie chimed in. "It took a while, but Fran figured it out—"

"The cloth is a portal!" they blurted out in unison.

Fran glared at her younger brother. "Yes, thank you, Charlie," she said. "I didn't want him to come along, by the way. He insisted on it."

Milly just stared at them. "How…" She threw her hands up in the air. "What?" Then she noticed that Father Alexiou was trying to slink away. "Where do you think you're going, Father Alexiou?" she demanded. "If that's even your real name."

"You— you have no power over me!" he stammered, gathering his bearings and standing a little straighter. "You're just a little girl! And I… I am the all-powerful Deimos Asgard!" He laughed like a hyena while the group stared at him in disbelief. "Ha…" He stopped laughing and began backing away toward the arched doorway. "Oops."

"You stole Athena's Shawl!" Milly shouted.

"Or tried to steal it," Faramund interjected. "Seems like your plan kind of failed, huh, Deimos?"

"You kidnapped my mother!" Milly saw red and hurtled herself toward Deimos Asgard, unsure of what she was going to do without a weapon, but certain as the sun shone that she was going to make him feel as much pain as he'd caused her. Before she could reach him, though, Fran and Charlie grabbed her by both arms. She struggled as they held her back, shouting, "What are you doing? Let go of me! He took our mum!"

"Milly! You don't know what that man is capable of," Fran said. "He might hurt you!"

"What do you mean, he took Mum?" Charlie asked.

"Why are you so strong?" Milly said, looking at Charlie. The hold he had on her arm was unsettling for an eight-year-old. She could barely process what was happening. So many things had happened so fast.

"Come on, guys!" she shouted at Mirabel and the others. "Help me!"

"Milly…" Mirabel said, holding her hands out, much like someone approaching a wild animal. "We need to retreat. We need to come up with a plan. Now, I'm doing this for your own good, okay?" She quickly picked Milly up and threw her over her shoulder. Milly began pounding on Mirabel's back with her fists, kicking and screaming for her to let her go. Meanwhile, Deimos Asgard was laughing maniacally, and Catalina, Faramund, Wolfstan, and King Jason stood completely lost without their weapons. They followed Mirabel and the struggling Milly through the temple and back outside. Fran and Charlie were right behind them, with Louie running alongside.

Once outside, Fran took the torn piece of Athena's Shawl out of her pocket and held it up to the sunlight.

"Okay…" she said, eyeing Milly nervously. "How are we going to do this? Charlie," she handed the picture of their parents standing in front of the house to her brother, "grab Louie, okay? And then hold this up so the cloth can catch the shadows being projected from the picture."

"Got it," Charlie said, bending over to pick up Louie.

"Wait!" Milly shouted, her voice growing hoarse. "Don't you want to save Mum?"

"We can come back, Milly," Fran told her as Charlie, with Louie squirming in his arms, tried to angle the picture frame just right in front of the cloth. "We know how to use the portal now."

"Once we get our weapons back, we can fight Deimos Asgard," Mirabel added, setting Milly down but not letting go of her wrist. "But right now, you need to go back home. Your father must be worried sick."

"I'm not leaving without Mum!" Milly protested.

"We don't even know where your mother is," Catalina said. "We need to regroup. Your mother will be okay. I promise."

"How do you know that?" Milly asked, as Fran took hold of her other hand and pulled her in front of the torn piece of cloth.

"The priest must need her for something," Catalina replied. "He won't hurt her, Milly."

Milly could tell that Catalina was trying to keep her voice steady. She was trying to make it seem like everything would be okay. But Milly had a horrible feeling that nothing would be okay. Her mother was on borrowed time, and Catalina and the others knew it. Her heart pounded so hard that she could feel the vibrations in her skull.

Charlie, while holding up the picture of their parents, took Milly's other hand. The cloth sucked the three siblings and their dog into it, and Captain Catalina, King Jason, Wolfstan, Faramund, and Mirabel watched as it vanished once again.

~

Milly landed on the floor of her bedroom, feeling just about ready to throttle her siblings. "How could you?!" she shouted, tears streaming down her face.

"Milly," Fran said, "please calm down. How do you even know for sure that that strange man took Mum?"

"Don't tell me to calm down!" Louie was barking up a storm, which only made matters worse. In a way, though, Milly felt more supported by him than by her siblings. "Wow," she said, "it's almost like Louie is the only one who cares besides me! Mum was there, somewhere! We could have looked for her! We could have saved her!"

"Like I said, we can go back." Fran gritted her teeth and gestured at Athena's Shawl, which was still hanging in the bedroom window. "What were you going to do? Start attacking that evil priest bloke without a plan?"

"That would have been better than doing nothing!" Milly said. She took a deep breath, trying to calm herself down a little. She couldn't, though. She was absolutely fuming. She heard a knock at her door and did the best she could to compose herself. "Come in," she said.

Her dad poked his head into the room, looking a bit puzzled. "What's all the shouting about?" he asked. "Why are you three sitting on the floor?"

"Um, hey, Dad," Fran stammered, glancing nervously at Milly. "We, uh, went on a little adventure."

John Martin raised an eyebrow. "What kind of adventure, exactly? Milly..." He gave his eldest daughter a strange look. "What are you wearing?"

Milly looked down at her clothes. She was still clad in the robe and sandals she had stolen from the unlucky villager girl. Not only that, but she was still holding her mother's necklace in her fist. So, that really just happened, she thought to herself. I'm not losing my mind. This is for real.

She began to cry, wanting, more than anything, to throw herself into her mother's arms. Now, because of Fran and Charlie, she wouldn't be able to. Not for a while, at least. Louie, sensing Milly's frustration, ran up to her and began to give her big kisses.

"Oh! Sweetheart," her father crouched down next to her. "What's the matter? Can you tell me what happened?"

Milly couldn't hold it back any longer. "Dad, an evil priest named Deimos Asgard kidnapped Mum! I... I found Athena's Shawl in Mum's closet," she pointed to the white cloth hanging in the window. "I could have saved her, but Fran and Charlie decided to bring us back home without doing anything!"

John Martin looked confused. He brushed Milly's hair behind her ears and exchanged glances with Fran and Charlie. "Why is she so upset?" he asked them. "What sort of make-believe game have you kids been playing? I don't like the sound of it."

"It's not make-believe, Dad!" Milly said, stifling a sob. "Louie found Mum's necklace in Deimos Asgard's pocket. Look!" She held it up to show him.

"Oh my goodness," Fran said, letting out a small gasp. Milly could tell that she was starting to believe her. Louie started whimpering again, and Charlie made a face like he was about to cry. For a moment, Milly's father almost looked like he was starting to believe her, too. As he examined the necklace closely, a crease appeared between his eyebrows. He reached down to take it from Milly, carefully rubbing his fingers over the blue pendant.

"Where did you get this?" he asked seriously.

"I just told you," Milly said, her heart sinking into her stomach. She took a deep breath and tried to explain things as clearly as she could. "That cloth I found in Mum's closet is an ancient artefact, and, as Fran

59

and Charlie discovered, it seems to be some sort of… portal to another world. The world in *War of the Ages 2*, in fact. I found Mum's necklace in the world that the cloth led to. Well, actually, as I said, Louie found it in the evil priest's pocket." She quickly told him the story that Mirabel and the others had shared with her — about Deimos Asgard trying to steal Athena's Shawl years ago, and the cloth disappearing altogether. "Somehow, Athena's Shawl ended up here," she said. "I don't know how, and I don't know why, but—"

"What, that old thing?" John Martin stood up and made his way over to the now-torn cloth. "Why have you ripped it?" he asked. "This was one of your mother's things. The day she went missing, I found it lying on the bed, so I put it in her closet for her. You know how she likes to go shopping—"

"I know it's hard to believe, Dad," Milly told him. "But we're not playing a game here. That cloth—no matter how Mum acquired it—is Athena's Shawl. It's an ancient artefact with mysterious powers. We actually learned about it in history class a few months ago."

"Milly, stop talking nonsense," her father said. "This isn't funny. Your mother is missing. You kids shouldn't be making a game out of it."

Milly shook her head in disbelief. "Are you even listening to me?" She looked at Fran and Charlie, pleading with her eyes for a little help. "Maybe you two can show him how the portal works," she said. "Did you rip the corner from Athena's Shawl so that you could bring us back here, Fran? That was good thinking. Louie and I must have been gone for quite a while." Though it didn't feel like they'd been gone for long, now that they were back. Milly wasn't sure, though. She was, frankly, quite discombobulated by the whole experience.

Her sister shook her head. "You and Louie weren't gone for all that long. Maybe Athena's Shawl makes time work differently... I don't know. Still, though, we knew something was off because you left your game unattended."

"Right," Milly said. "That's a good point. In that world, it had been a couple of days. But it seems like I was only gone for a few hours in this world, huh?"

Fran rocked back and forth on her feet, nodding vigorously. "We also brought this picture of Mum, Dad, and the house into the portal with us," she said. "Because it seems like, whatever image you project onto Athena's Shawl, that's where it takes you. As long as there's light being shone through it—and we have the image of wherever we want to go on hand—we should be able to go anywhere." She shrugged. "At least, in theory."

Milly's father crossed his arms, a stern expression on his face. "This is absurd. I won't entertain such fantasies. We need to focus on finding your mother through proper means."

"But Dad, it's real!" Charlie insisted, pointing at the necklace dangling from his father's fingers. "That was the necklace Mum was wearing the day she went missing, right?"

"Uh... it sure looks a lot like it, doesn't it?" John Martin said, examining the necklace again. "Are you sure you're not playing a joke, guys? Because if so, you're taking it way too far."

Fran took a deep breath, trying to find the right words. "Dad, we know it sounds crazy, but we wouldn't joke about Mum."

Milly stepped in, grateful for the support of her siblings. "We're just trying to find her, Dad. We thought maybe this could help."

Her father sighed, clearly frustrated. "I appreciate your concern, but some quote-unquote magical shawl isn't going to bring your mother back."

"It's starting to get dark," Milly said, noticing that the sun wasn't shining through Athena's Shawl anymore. "We've already wasted too much time."

"Huh," John Martin said. He looked like he was trying not to roll his eyes, which irked Milly. "Well, that's convenient, isn't it? Come on, guys, let's just—"

"Wait!" Charlie piped up, his face brightening. "Wait just a minute! I have an idea." He ran off to his bedroom, returning seconds later with his Spider-Man nightlight. "Maybe, if we plug this into the wall, we can hold the cloth in front of it. Then, we'll be able to project Milly's computer game onto it, right?"

"Charlie! That's brilliant!" Milly exclaimed. "We can plug it in over here." She took the nightlight from Charlie and plugged it into the outlet beneath the window ledge. It cast a warm light across the room— a light so bright, in fact, that it hurt Milly's eyes. "For goodness' sake, Charlie, how do you sleep with this thing?"

Charlie shrugged. "Well… don't tell anyone, but I'm still afraid of the dark."

"That's okay," Milly said, tousling his hair. "This is going to work perfectly! I just know it!" She grabbed Athena's Shawl from where it was hanging in the window and held it up in front of Charlie's nightlight. The fabric absorbed the light, and immediately, the shadows of the three children, their father, and their dog started to dance across it. Louie growled at the shifting shadows, still unsure of the whole Athena's Shawl situation—as was Milly, for that matter. What if there came a time when they couldn't return after using the shawl to enter another world? There was so much they still didn't understand about it, but there was no time for doubts. Her mother was somewhere out there, and Milly was going to find her.

"Fran," Milly said, "do you think you can tilt my computer screen a little so it faces Athena's Shawl?"

"Yep," Fran replied, rushing over to Milly's computer. She adjusted the screen until, slowly but surely, *War of the Ages 2* began to project onto the fabric. As before, the image was mostly shadows and hints of colour—not the clearest projection, but it would do. "There!" Fran said. "Is it working?"

Athena's Shawl began to undulate slightly. Milly hadn't noticed it doing that the first time. The shadows of the characters being projected onto the fabric began to emit a faint glow. Once again, Milly felt like the shawl was calling to her in some strange way.

"I think so!" Milly said. "See, Dad? We told you!"

By now, John Martin's earlier stern expression had faltered. All the while, he had been trying to figure out how to stop his eldest daughter from getting wrapped up in her game, thinking it was just some fantasy. But now, seeing the scene unfold before him, everything he had been thinking was quickly replaced by a mixture of awe and disbelief. "How... how is this possible?"

Fran smiled, a glimmer of triumph in her eyes. "We told you, Dad," she echoed Milly. "Athena's Shawl is a portal. We can use it to project images and travel to different places. According to Milly, this is where Mum went."

Milly's father, though still processing the surreal scene unfolding before him, couldn't deny the evidence. There really was something magical about the odd piece of fabric he'd found on his wife's side of the bed months ago. "I... I don't understand," he said.

"Trust me," Milly said, beaming. "I thought it was weird, too, at first. Actually, I still think it's weird."

"I think it's cool," Fran said, stepping closer to the cloth.

"Wait a minute! Wait.' their father said, grabbing Fran by the wrist. "If that really is a portal to another world—I can't believe I'm even saying this right now," he said, running his other hand through his thinning hair. "This is crazy. I won't allow you to go back through it. It's too dangerous."

"But, Dad—" Fran began, trying to protest.

"No buts," he said, shaking his head. "What will you do if you can't get back? You may have gotten lucky the first time, but you can't predict what might happen this time around."

"What about Mum?" Milly folded her arms across her chest. "Are we just going to leave her there?"

"If your mum is in there, it's not your responsibility to get her back," he replied. "We... we need to hire a special investigator, someone who knows how to handle paranormal objects, parallel dimensions, and all that." He unplugged Charlie's nightlight, and the room went dim. The faint projections from *War of the Ages 2* vanished, making Milly want to start crying again. They had worked so hard to convince their dad, but he was still too scared to truly believe them—too terrified of losing everything.

"I'm going to take this, for now," he said, grabbing Athena's Shawl and shoving it into his pocket. "I'll take it to a paranormal investigator as soon as I can. Okay? Now, what do you lot want for dinner?"

"I'm not hungry," Milly said, her voice hollow with defeat. "Can everyone get out of my room, please?"

"Milly..." her father began, but she cut him off.

"I said 'Get out of my room!' Just leave me alone, already!" She curled up in the middle of her bed. Louie, sensing her distress, jumped up to lay next to her and let out a deep sigh, clearly exhausted from the strange adventure. Milly scratched him behind his ear, and tears began to fall again. "Get out," she whispered, the words barely audible. "Please."

Without another word, John Martin quietly ushered Milly's younger siblings out of the room. "I'll let you know when dinner's ready," he said, then gently closed the door behind him.

Chapter 6
When Worlds Collide

The next morning, Milly woke with a fire in her belly and a plan forming in her mind. Louie had slept on her bed, which was comforting. She supposed they had bonded in a special way. Sitting up, she ran her fingers through her hair and glanced at the window where Athena's Shawl had been hanging less than eight hours earlier. She still couldn't believe her dad had taken it away from her. While she understood he was just trying to keep her safe, she couldn't help but resent him for it. She'd decided: she was going to enlist her friends' help, steal back Athena's Shawl from her dad, and save her mother once and for all—no matter the cost.

She got out of bed, walked over to her computer, and minimised *War of the Ages 2*. Afraid to exit the game completely—now knowing the characters were, at least in theory, living, breathing people—she opened her Discord account in a new window. Her group chat with Ashley and Lucy was already lit up with notifications from the night before. Absentmindedly, she nibbled on a cracker from the plate she'd fixed the previous day. It was stale but still edible.

"Hey, where are you?" Ashley had messaged. "I thought we were going to play tonight. Are you okay?"

Lucy's message was less empathetic: "Milly, if you're flaking out on us, just say so."

"Sorry!" Milly typed back. "I wasn't flaking out. Something bloody insane happened last night."

She started getting ready for school but paused when she heard the Discord notification chime. Sitting back down at her desk, she felt a mix of excitement and nerves as she prepared to share the events of the previous evening.

"What happened?" Ashley replied.

Milly began typing furiously: everything about falling into the world of *War of the Ages 2*, meeting the characters they played almost daily, and finding her mother's necklace. Then she stopped, hesitating, and erased it all.

"I'll tell you at school," she finally sent. "It'll be better to explain in person."

She logged out of Discord, changed into her uniform, and went downstairs to grab some breakfast.

Her dad was at the kitchen table, sipping tea and reading the newspaper. Milly poured herself a bowl of cornflakes and sat across from him. He lowered the paper slightly, his expression carrying an unspoken apology.

"Morning," he said. "Are you still angry with me?"

Milly didn't answer. In that moment, she wanted nothing to do with him. Guilt tugged at her, though—not just for her silence but for the fact she was planning to steal Athena's Shawl back. Even though she believed it was the right thing to do, she hated the idea of deceiving him.

Where would he be keeping it? she wondered. I'll get Ash and Lucy to help me search his bedroom after school.

"You're giving me the silent treatment, huh?" John Martin said, folding his newspaper. "That's fine, Milly. I understand you think I'm being unfair, but you'll come around."

Once again, Milly said nothing. She finished her cereal, grabbed her schoolbag from the foyer, gave Louie a Louie chewie while kissing him on the top of his head, and left for school.

~

"Okay, you guys won't believe what happened last night," she began as Ashley and Lucy joined her at their usual picnic table. They were having fish and chips for lunch, and Milly, as usual, had bought a can of Red Bull from the vending machine. The words tumbled out fast and jumbled from her mouth — probably because she'd had too much caffeine — but she could hardly contain her excitement. "So, do you remember how I brought up Athena's Shawl yesterday? I asked if you guys thought it could be real. Well," she said, not waiting for an answer, "it is real. I found it in my mum's closet, and it turns out it's some kind of portal."

"A portal?" Ashley asked. "Milly—"

"Louie fell into the portal," Milly said, steamrolling right over Ashley's question. "And then I fell in after him. War of the Ages 2 was being projected onto Athena's Shawl because I hung it up in the window to get rid of the glare from the sun. My sister thinks that, as long as you hold Athena's Shawl in front of a light source and project an image of a place onto it, you can travel to any world or time you want. Actually, it was a little unclear if I was physically in another world or if I had time-travelled back to medieval times—"

"Wait," Lucy said, putting her hand up. "Slow down, Milly. What are you talking about?"

"The reason I couldn't play War of the Ages 2 with you guys last night is that I fell into the world of War of the Ages 2. I know it sounds crazy," she said, noticing the perplexed looks on her friends' faces. "But it's true. I met the War of the Ages characters — Wolfstan, Mirabel, and everyone. I thought it was a dream at first, but—"

"The dog fell in! Yeah, I'm pretty sure that's a dream," Lucy said. "I mean, come on. You had Athena's Shawl on your mind yesterday, and you play War of the Ages almost every day. It makes sense that you'd have a dream like that."

68

"Well, if you'd let me finish talking," Milly said, a bit annoyed. "I could explain how I know it's not a dream."

"Wait, okay, so," Ashley said, looking a little concerned. "How do you know that what you found in your mum's closet is Athena's Shawl? Why would there be an ancient artefact in your mum's closet?"

"I have no idea," Milly told her. "My dad said he found it on their bed the day she went missing. He put it in her closet, assuming she'd just gone on a shopping spree or something."

"Okay, but…" Ashley hesitated, clearly at a loss for words. Milly could tell that neither she nor Lucy believed her.

"I knew you guys wouldn't believe me," she said. "Which is why you've got to come to my house after school and help me look for Athena's Shawl in my parents' bedroom." She took another sip from her Red Bull. "Unfortunately, my dad took it away last night. He says he wants to take it to a paranormal investigator."

"Milly, I'm about to take away your Red Bull," Lucy said. "You've got to be joking with us."

"I'm not joking!" she said. "Come on. Just help me look for it. I found something in the War of the Ages world that really freaked me out."

"What did you find?" Ashley asked.

"My mother's necklace," Milly told her. "The one she was wearing the day she went missing. I think she fell into Athena's Shawl — just like I did — and got kidnapped by an evil priest."

"An evil priest?"

"Yep," she said, relieved to have told someone the whole story. She popped a piece of fried fish into her mouth and crunched up her empty Red Bull can in her fist. "His name is Deimos Asgard, but he was going by a different name — probably to keep his true identity a secret. Louie found my mum's necklace in his pocket, and he seemed awfully interested in Athena's Shawl, so now I'm thinking, 'Huh. Maybe my mum is connected to Athena's Shawl somehow.'"

"This is so weird," Lucy said, finally digging into her lunch. "Okay, I'll bite."

"Me, too," Ashley said. "I know you wouldn't lie about your mum, Milly."

"Thank you," Milly said, beaming. "I'll prove to you guys that it's real. We just need to steal back Athena's Shawl from my dad, first. Luckily, he'll be at work all day, so it shouldn't be too difficult."

"You said your sister knows about it, too, right?" Lucy asked.

"Yep. And my brother. They're the ones who brought me back to the real world… or, this particular world, I guess. I think both worlds are real."

"Are you going to tell Harry and Chris?" Ashley said. "Maybe they could help us."

"Um… I don't know…" Milly mulled it over. "Harry would probably say that I'm making it all up."

"To be fair, I kind of think you're making it all up," Lucy said, polishing off her fish and chips. "But, I'm intrigued. So, I'll give you the chance to prove that it's real."

"Gee, thanks," Milly said, a bit sheepishly. "If we can successfully get Athena's Shawl back from my dad, then I'll tell the boys. For now, they don't need to know. If they wanted to know, they should have eaten lunch with us!"

"Well, Harry is eating with his other friends, and Chris always goes wherever Harry goes," Ashley said. "You know how it is."

"Yeah…" Milly sighed. "I just think we're far more interesting than the guys on the football team. But whatever."

A few hours later, school let out, and Milly, Ashley, and Lucy set off for Milly's house. Fran and Charlie would be taking the bus home, so they would have the house to themselves for an hour or so. Not that it mattered — Fran and Charlie seemed on board with the whole Athena's Shawl situation — but Milly was thankful for the chance to show her friends how the magical shawl worked on her own. She unlocked the front door, greeted Louie, who had run to see who had arrived, and the girls then set their bags down. Lucy and Ashley seemed keen to find out what Milly had been going on about during lunch.

Lucy, who tended to act like she owned the place whenever she went over to Milly's house, strutted into the kitchen and started raiding the fridge. "What sort of snacks have you got?" she asked. "I could murder a ham and mustard sandwich right now." Louie, hearing the sound of the fridge, ran up to Lucy and pawed at her to give him a treat, which she did, as usual. Louie always ran to the fridge every time it was opened and knew everyone loved spoiling him.

"You can make one if you like," Milly said, slightly irritated that Lucy was more interested in eating than looking for Athena's Shawl. "Just be quick about it. Ash and I will start looking for Athena's Shawl in my dad's bedroom." Ashley nodded, and together, they clomped up the stairs. Milly tried the handle on her parents' bedroom door, only to discover that it was locked.

"I can't believe it," she said, a bit taken aback. "My dad's locked the door. He usually trusts us enough to keep it unlocked."

"Well, he's keeping something valuable in there now, isn't he?" Ashley asked. "Is there… any way we can pick the lock?"

"I've never picked a lock before," Milly said. "Have you?"

Ashley shook her head. Just then, Lucy came traipsing up the stairs, holding half a ham and mustard sandwich, followed by Louie, who was looking at the appetising treat and licking his lips.

"You couldn't have waited two minutes?" Lucy asked. "Why are you just standing outside the door?"

"My dad locked it," Milly told her. "Do you know how to pick a lock, Lucy?"

Lucy took a big bite from her sandwich and licked a bit of mustard off her fingers. "I can give it a try," she said with her mouth full. "I've seen loads of films where people pick locks. Does either one of you have a hair grip or something?"

Milly and Ashley looked at each other. Without saying another word, Ashley carefully took out one of her kirby grips and handed it to Lucy.

"Perfect!" Lucy said, wolfing down the rest of her sandwich. "Now, I'll just need a screwdriver. Does your dad keep one somewhere, Milly?"

Louie felt disappointed he hadn't been offered another treat and gave a little sigh.

Milly nodded. "Yeah, he has a toolbox in the garage. I can grab a screwdriver from there. Let's give it a shot!" The three girls hurried down the stairs and out into the garage. The air was thick with the smell of sawdust and petrol. Milly approached the toolbox in the corner and opened it, revealing a screwdriver, some sandpaper, and a rusty tape measure. She grabbed the screwdriver and handed it to Lucy, who couldn't have looked more overjoyed. The three of them ran back upstairs, excited to see whether they'd actually be able to pull this off.

"Okay," Lucy said. "We just need to insert the screwdriver into the lock and use Ashley's hair grip to move the pins. In movies, they just kind of jiggle it around until they hear a click." Lucy paused, looking a bit nervous. "Sounds simple enough, right?"

Once again, Milly felt a pang of guilt for trying to break into her dad's bedroom — but she knew it was for the greater good. Lucy knelt in front of the door, inserted the screwdriver and hair grip into the lock, and began to manoeuvre it delicately.

"Be careful, Lucy," Milly whispered nervously. "I don't want you to accidentally break something."

Lucy shot her a confident smile. "Relax. I got this." She focused on the task at hand, jiggling the screwdriver and hair grip in the lock. After a few tense moments, there was a faint click, and Milly's eyes widened in surprise.

"Did you do it?" Ashley asked.

Lucy grinned, holding up the screwdriver. She returned the kirby grip to Ashley, who used it to clip her fringe back, and turned the knob to open the door. "I did! Ladies, we have a successfully picked lock!"

Milly couldn't believe their luck. "Wow, Lucy, you're amazing!"

Lucy stood up, brushing off her hands on her school uniform. "Well, I do watch a lot of spy movies. Now, let's see if we can find this mysterious shawl of yours." She waltzed right in, dropping the screwdriver on the floor, and kneeled to look under the bed. "Nope. Not under there."

Milly started rifling through her mum's closet, though she didn't think her dad would have put Athena's Shawl back in the same place he left it last time. It would have been too obvious, and her dad was smarter than that. Feeling a bit awkward, she reached under her dad's pillow, then her mum's, but came up empty-handed.

"Where could it be?" she said. "You don't think he took it with him to work, do you?"

"Well, he locked his door, didn't he?" Lucy said. "He must be trying to hide something. Any luck over there, Ash?"

Ashley was looking through Milly's dad's desk drawer — which was a mess of paperwork, elastic bands, and other miscellaneous office supplies. "Nope," Ashley said. "I feel like we're looking in really obvious places, though." She turned to face Milly, who was frantically digging through her dad's dresser. "Think carefully, Milly," she said. "Where would your dad keep something that he doesn't want anyone to find? Like, where would you never think to look?"

"Hmm…" Milly thought for a moment. There was a music box that her dad kept on his bedside table — a Christmas gift from her mum. "Maybe…" she said. "Maybe he hid it in plain sight." She rushed over to the music box and opened it, and — sure enough — muffling the beautiful twinkling of *Für Elise*, was Athena's Shawl, folded neatly into a tight square. "I found it!" Milly said. "I can't believe I actually found it!" She took it out of the music box and unfolded it to show her friends. "See? Doesn't it look just like how Mr. Hayes described it?"

"Huh…" Lucy said, tilting her head to the side. "Yeah. It's actually a bit uncanny. Still, though, I feel like your mum could have gotten that at a charity shop or something."

"You wouldn't catch my mum dead at a charity shop," Milly said. "I mean, it's not like she's all that posh, but she's too posh to go charity shopping."

"Did someone rip it?" Lucy asked. "It looks a bit roughed up."

"Fran ripped the corner off of it so that she could bring me back home," Milly explained. "Actually, come to think of it, Fran probably still has the corner. We could have just used that."

"Yeah, but I don't want to wait," Ashley said, practically bouncing up and down. "Will you show us how it works now? Can we

74

transport ourselves to the world of *War of the Ages 2*?" All the while, Louie was staring up at the cloth in hope.

"You want to come with us, Louie?" Milly asked the little dog. Louie wagged his tail and barked happily. "I think that's a yes," she said, turning to her friends. "Louie was quite helpful when we went into Athena's Shawl the first time. Actually…" She arched an eyebrow and tapped her foot at him. "He's kind of the reason I got into this mess in the first place."

"Oh, let's bring him along," Ashley said. "He'd be good protection, don't you think?"

Lucy scoffed. "Louie couldn't hurt a fly," she said. "But, sure… bring the dog."

"We're bringing his leash this time, though," Milly said to Louie. She grinned at Ashley and Lucy. "He tends to run off."

After grabbing Louie's leash from where it hung by a hook in the foyer, the girls reconvened in Milly's bedroom. Milly excitedly grabbed two pieces of scotch tape from her desk drawer, and began to tape Athena's Shawl up in the window — just like she did last time. "Good thing it's sunny, today," she said. "I can't wait for you two to meet the War of the Ages characters." She paused for a moment. "Well… Faramund and Wolfstan can be a bit abrasive, but you'll love Mirabel, Ash. She's quite nice." Louie jumped up onto Milly's bed, and Ashley scratched him behind the ear and gave him a Louie chewie while Lucy helped Milly set up War of the Ages 2 on her computer.

"This is bonkers," Ashley said. Louie barked, as if in agreement. "I can't believe we're about to go inside of a computer game."

"I'll believe it when I see it," Lucy said. "I still think Milly's full of it."

Milly punched her lightly on the shoulder. "You'll see soon enough, won't you? Now, be patient. We have to wait for the sun to hit the shawl just right so that it catches the shadows and shapes coming from my computer screen." The room fell into a momentary silence as they continued to watch the sun's light creep through the thin white fabric of Athena's Shawl. Finally, Milly stood up. "Alright, it's time. Everyone, gather around."

The girls and Louie huddled close to the window, their eyes glued to the shawl. Milly, with a confident grin, pressed a button on her computer, and the game's loading screen appeared.

"Here goes nothing," Milly said, taking a deep breath. "On the count of three. One... two... three!"

At that moment, Athena's Shawl caught the sunlight just right, the familiar shadows from War of the Ages 2 dancing upon the white surface of the cloth. All three girls felt a strange sensation as if they were being pulled into the cloth. Milly, feeling a bit nervous, clipped Louie's leash to his collar and scooped him up into her arms. "This is it," she said to her friends. "Brace yourselves!"

Lucy, usually bold and brazen, looked a little scared. "Oh my goodness," she said. "What the —"

Ashley, to Milly's surprise, was practically jumping up and down in excitement. "Oh my goodness! I can't *believe* this!"

Moments later, they were sprawling on the mossy ground in the overgrown forest — exactly where Milly landed the first time she and Louie entered Athena's Shawl. She set Louie down on the ground, wrapping hold of his leash around her wrist and listening closely for any signs of danger. Faramund had mentioned that the goddess, Nemesis, would be back at some point. Milly wasn't really sure what that meant, or when Nemesis would be back, but it made her wary. She got up from the forest floor and brushed herself off before turning to look at her friends, who were looking rather dazed by the whole experience.

"Where…" Lucy grunted and lifted herself from the ground. "Where are we?"

"Uh… short answer?" Milly said. "We're in *War of the Ages 2*. Or Ancient Greece. Or both."

"No *way*," Ashley said, her face brightening as she looked around the forest. "See, I wasn't sure if you were serious, Milly, but this… this is…" she trailed off.

Milly helped her up, her heart, once again, thumping like a drum in her chest. "I know," she said, as Ashley brushed off her school uniform. "I know it's crazy. It's… going to take some getting used to, to say the least." She was starting to wonder how she was going to find Mirabel, Captain Catalina, and the others. *The village would probably be a good place to start looking*, she thought to herself. *I wonder what they've been up to.*

"Okay, so…" Lucy said, still half-dazed. She reached down to pet Louie, who was sniffing at a nearby patch of flowers. "What do we do now?"

"There's a village, not too far from here," Milly said. "I *think* I know how to get there…"

"You *think*?" Lucy looked a bit sceptical.

Milly glanced at Louie, and her face brightened a bit. "I'll bet Louie knows where it is," she said. "There are loads of interesting smells in the village, right Louie?"

~

The girls followed Louie as he eagerly trotted ahead, sniffing at the strange and unfamiliar scents of the mossy statues lining the path.

The air was thick with the earthy aroma of the ancient forest, mingling with the faint smell of incense from distant altars. The atmosphere was both serene and tense, a feeling Milly couldn't shake — like something important was about to happen.

"Where do you think we are, exactly?" Ashley asked, her eyes scanning the surroundings. "It looks like it's from the game, but... everything feels so real."

"I know, right?" Milly said, feeling both exhilarated and cautious. "I think we're in the world of *War of the Ages 2*, but it's... it's not a game anymore. This is real. Well, as real as it can get for us."

Lucy, still a little disoriented, kept looking around like she was expecting someone to jump out at them. "If we run into any of those mythical creatures, I'm out of here."

"Don't worry," Milly said, her voice steady, though her pulse quickened. "I'll protect you. Plus, we have Louie."

Louie barked again, more energetically now, as if he understood the conversation. He padded along with purpose, heading down the narrow, winding trail that seemed to lead them further into the heart of the forest. Milly could see patches of sunlight filtering through the thick canopy above, casting dancing shadows on the mossy ground.

As they walked, Milly found herself glancing around, trying to familiarize herself with the scenery. She had spent hours exploring the world in the game, but this place felt more alive, more immediate. There were birds calling from unseen branches, the whisper of wind through leaves, and a faint sound of rushing water in the distance.

"There it is," Milly said, pointing ahead. They came to a clearing, and through the trees, the outline of a small village appeared. The stone buildings were simple, but there was a warmth to the place. People were milling about, some of them dressed in armour, others in robes, their movements purposeful.

Milly felt a sudden rush of excitement. "That's the village! We'll find Mirabel, Faramund, and the others there. They've got to be around."

Ashley's eyes widened. "No way... this is really happening."

Lucy shook her head, still processing everything. "I'm going to need a minute to catch up with all this." She shot Milly a look. "But, alright, let's go. Lead the way."

Louie barked again, as though urging them to hurry. Milly grinned, pulling on his leash gently. "Let's go, then."

They walked toward the village, the sounds of life growing louder as they approached. Milly's heart raced with anticipation. This was their chance to meet the characters from the game, to discover more about Athena's Shawl, and maybe even uncover more about her mum's disappearance. It felt like everything was aligning, and she couldn't help but feel that this was just the beginning of something bigger.

"These statues are freaking me out," Ashley said.

"I know, right?" Milly said. "Do you recognise them?"

"Yep. They're uh… very lifelike. I think I prefer them pixelated."

"They're just statues, Ash," Lucy said, although she looked a bit creeped out herself. "They're not going to hurt you."

"Wait a minute," Ashley stopped in the middle of the path. Louie whimpered and started nudging at the back of her knees with his nose as if urging her to keep moving forward. "Did you guys hear that?"

"What?" Milly asked, and then, suddenly, she heard it too. A faint whispering, almost like the wind, but not quite. The girls exchanged uneasy glances as the whispering began to grow louder. Milly clutched

Louie's leash tighter as the statues along the path seemed to shift in their mossy stillness.

"I don't like this," Lucy said, her eyes darting nervously between the statues.

Before anyone could say anything else, the statues began to tremble, their stony exteriors cracking open. One by one, they stepped down from their pedestals, the eerie whispering now forming discernible words.

"We are the guardians of the temple that stands within the forest," they said in deep, gravelly voices. "We command you to leave this place at once!" The statues started to move towards them, slowly, but surely. Milly, Ashley, Lucy, and Louie took several steps back, their eyes full of fear and disbelief. The statues surrounded them, creating a tight circle. Panic set in, but just as Milly opened her mouth to scream, an arrow zipped past them, narrowly missing Lucy's head before embedding itself into the eye of the statue closest to them.

Milly turned around to see Wolfstan with another arrow at the ready. Captain Catalina, King Jason, Mirabel, and Faramund were close behind him, determination etched on their faces as they drew their weapons.

"Stay out of the way, Milly!" Captain Catalina commanded. "We'll handle this!"

With a battle cry, King Jason charged forward, swinging his sword at one of the statues, and chipping away at the hard surface. Mirabel brandished her own sword, and in just a few swift movements, caused the statue closest to her to crumble into dust.

"I didn't realise these things were alive!" Faramund said, brandishing his weapon and standing back-to-back with Mirabel.

"Yeah, this place is full of surprises," Mirabel said.

Milly, Ashley, and Lucy scurried into the bushes nearby to hide. Louie followed them, his tail tucked between his legs. "Oh, wow!" Ashley said, watching through the brush in awe. "Is that really Mirabel? She's so cool!"

All of a sudden, Louie, apparently gaining some courage, darted out from the bushes. He pulled so hard that Milly couldn't hold onto his leash. "*Louie Roi!*" She called after him. "Not again!"

"Louie, no!" Milly cried, her heart racing as she watched her dog darting fearlessly between the statues' legs. She couldn't believe her little dog was being so brave — or so reckless.

"Don't worry, Milly," Ashley said, grinning with excitement. "Look at him go! He's distracting them!"

"I'm glad *he's* excited about this," Milly said, her voice tinged with nervousness, but she couldn't help but smile at Louie's bravery. "But I swear, he's going to get us all killed one of these days."

Lucy's eyes were wide with wonder. "This is insane," she murmured. "It's like something straight out of an action movie."

As Louie nipped at the statues' stone ankles, distracting them, Captain Catalina and King Jason pressed forward with precision, each strike bringing down the statues piece by piece. The sound of cracking stone echoed in the air as Mirabel and Faramund worked in perfect sync to finish the statues off.

One of the statues collapsed into dust with a loud, satisfying crash, and another fell forward into the ground with a heavy thud. The guardian statues, now defeated, crumbled around them.

"Good job, team!" Wolfstan shouted, lowering his bow, which he still held at the ready. He had a look of approval on his face as he surveyed the destruction.

"Thanks for the save, Wolfstan," Milly called out, rushing to catch up with Louie, who was happily wagging his tail as he trotted back to her. "You guys are amazing!"

"Don't mention it," Captain Catalina said, wiping the sweat from her brow as she sheathed her sword. "This place has many secrets and a tendency to throw unexpected challenges at us. But we're used to it."

Mirabel approached Milly, giving her a warm smile. "It's good to see you again, Milly. And I see you've brought some friends. I'm glad you all made it here safely."

Ashley practically bounced on her feet. "You're Mirabel! You're the coolest person ever! I can't believe we're meeting you in person!"

Mirabel laughed softly, her eyes twinkling with amusement. "I'm just doing my job. But it's good to know I have some fans."

Milly felt a mix of awe and relief wash over her. She had been so worried about finding them again, and now they were right there in front of her, helping her — and her friends — through the unknown. "Thanks, everyone. You've really saved us," she said, turning to Faramund, King Jason, and Captain Catalina.

"No problem," Faramund grinned, wiping some dust off his blade. "It's what we do. This place has always been full of strange happenings. You never know what's next."

"Exactly," said King Jason, his sword gleaming in the sunlight. "But we always handle it. Just remember, Milly, that *War of the Ages 2* isn't just a game. It's a world, and it can be dangerous, even for us."

Milly nodded, understanding the weight of his words. "I know. I won't forget that."

Lucy, who had been watching the exchange with wide eyes, suddenly spoke up. "So, uh, where are we heading next? Are we supposed to be doing something important?"

Mirabel turned to her with a serious expression. "There's always something important to do in this world. The temple, for example… and the goddess, Nemesis, might be back soon."

Milly's stomach tightened at the mention of Nemesis. "That's right… you said Nemesis would be back. Do you know when?"

Mirabel exchanged a glance with Captain Catalina. "Not exactly. But we should be prepared for her arrival. She doesn't take kindly to those who trespass in her domain."

"I guess we'd better get moving, then," Milly said, feeling a shiver run down her spine. "I'm not sure what Nemesis wants, but I have a feeling it's not going to be good for us."

"Agreed," said Wolfstan, his tone serious as he adjusted his quiver of arrows. "We should head to the temple. There are things happening here that we don't understand, but I'm sure Nemesis plays a big role in it."

"We'll help you, Milly," Ashley said, her voice filled with determination. "Whatever comes next, we're in this together."

Louie barked happily, as if agreeing. Milly smiled down at him and handed him a Louie chewie as a reward for his bravery, then turned to her friends. "Thanks, guys. I don't know what I'd do without you."

With the group united and ready for whatever lay ahead, they set off toward the temple — the shadows of the statues still lingering on the forest path as they moved forward into the unknown.

Ashley, who had been listening in with rapt attention, nudged Milly with her elbow. "Is this part of the game too?" she asked, a mix of excitement and bewilderment in her voice. "Or is this… real?"

Milly paused, considering. "I think this might be more than just a game now," she said, glancing around at her friends, who looked as equally awestruck as she felt. The forest, the village, the characters they

83

were meeting — everything felt too real. Too much like a world of its own.

Mirabel, walking just ahead, overheard their conversation. "It's always been real, Ashley," she said, her voice tinged with a hint of sadness. "This world, our lives, everything. We may have started as characters in a game, but we've been living in this reality for much longer than you think."

Chapter 7
The Plan

Milly caught up with Catalina, her friends, and Louie close at her heels. "Secret?" she asked. "What sort of secret?" The forest was beginning to thin around them as they made their way towards the small village. Milly's heart was pounding in her chest as she tried not to trip over Louie. "Did you find out where he's keeping my mum?"

Captain Catalina didn't reply immediately. She raised a finger to her lips, signalling Milly to remain silent. Her expression seemed to say: *We'll tell you everything in due time… just be patient.*

Milly's mind raced. *A secret tied to my mum,* she thought. *Could this be the break I've been waiting for?*

As they approached the village, Milly spotted the familiar stone walls encircling the small settlement in the distance. It was just as she remembered—tiny and bustling with merchants selling shiny trinkets and delicious-smelling meats. She noticed Louie licking his chops and tightened her grip on his lead. "We'll get you a little treat soon, boy," she told him. "Just give us a second to get settled in."

"That dog of yours…" King Jason remarked, eyeing Louie. "He's a bit spoiled, isn't he?"

"What makes you say that?" Milly retorted. Louie was indeed very much spoiled, but it was none of King Jason's business.

"So…" Ashley asked, walking beside Mirabel. "Where are we going, exactly?"

"We've been staying with a very nice woman and her daughter," Mirabel replied. "Their house is just up ahead."

The scent of freshly baked bread and the boisterous laughter of men stumbling around in front of a nearby bar filled the air. Louie barked at them, likely wanting to say "hello," but Milly tugged him away. "Some other time, boy," she said. It almost seemed like the men were laughing at them, though Milly couldn't be certain why.

As they walked through the village, more and more people began to notice them. Some children, about their age, pointed and laughed before scurrying away.

"Why is everyone looking at us?" Lucy asked. Milly wondered the same thing.

"Just ignore them," Mirabel said, hiding a small smile behind her hand. "We're nearly there."

Captain Catalina led the group to a modest house at the edge of the village. Made from sun-dried mud bricks with red clay tiles, it had a quaint charm. Milly found it quite appealing. A delectable smell wafted from the open window, and a plump, friendly-faced woman was tending to the garden out front.

When she noticed the group approaching, her face lit up. "Catalina!" she called, rushing over to greet them. "And Mirabel! It's been too long."

She stepped back, eyeing Milly, Ashley, and Lucy with suspicion. "And who are these young ones?"

Catalina smiled warmly. "This is Milly, Ashley, and Lucy," she said, gently encouraging the girls forward. Louie barked, as if to say, *Hey, what about me?* Catalina laughed. "And that's Louie, of course. Can't forget him."

"Alright..." the woman said, still looking slightly uncertain. "How do you know these children?" she asked. "And why are they wearing such strange clothing?"

86

"I'm afraid Milly's mother is missing," Catalina explained. Meanwhile, Milly, Ashley, and Lucy looked down at their school uniforms, feeling a bit embarrassed.

Why didn't I change back into what I was wearing yesterday? Milly thought to herself. No wonder everyone's staring at us. She had to admit she wasn't the best at planning.

"Your mother is missing?" The woman gave Milly a concerned look. "How awful! You must be worried sick."

"Yep," Catalina continued. "It seems that Milly's mum has found herself entangled in the affairs of…" She lowered her voice. "You-know-who."

"Mmm." The woman nodded solemnly and gestured for them to join her inside. "Come in, all of you. My daughter has prepared a lamb stew, and there are honey cakes for dessert. We have much to discuss."

Milly's stomach rumbled as they entered the little house. Lucy looked like she was regretting having eaten that ham and mustard sandwich back home.

A woman, slightly younger than Milly's mother, was hunched over an open fire in the centre of the room—a sight that was, frankly, a bit alarming. Milly quickly realised that this was probably just how people cooked during this time. Besides, there was a hole in the roof directly above the fire, allowing the smoke to escape. *That's pretty clever,* Milly thought.

The young woman was stirring a pot of chunky stew with a wooden spoon. She glanced up at them, gave a brief nod and smile, and returned to stirring.

"That's my daughter, Sophia," the older woman explained to Milly, Ashley, and Lucy. "She's mute, which means she's unable to speak. However, she can make an incredible lamb stew."

Sophia rolled her eyes at her mother, making Milly laugh. It was the sort of thing she might have done to her own mother if faced with a similar comment about one of her talents.

"And my name is Helen," the older woman added, bringing a hand to her chest. "I'm not much of a cook myself, but I grow all the herbs Sophia uses in her dishes. It's been difficult since my husband passed away..." She trailed off, her gaze growing distant for a moment. Then she smiled. "But we're quite proud of our little home."

"You have a lovely home," Ashley said, her eyes fixed on the golden honey cakes resting on the counter. "Thank you for inviting us in."

That was Ashley all over. Coming from a posh family, she knew how to be polite when the situation called for it.

Meanwhile, Louie had taken a keen interest in Sophia, jumping up and down in excitement—clearly more drawn to the lamb stew than to anything else. Sophia gasped and gently pushed him away. Holding up a finger, she dipped her spoon into the stew, blew on a thin strip of lamb, and tossed it to the floor for Louie.

Louie barked in delight, as if to say, *thank you,* and lunged at the morsel.

"Oh, thank you!" Milly said, clasping her hands together. "He appreciates it!"

Sophia nodded and stood up, brushing off her hands. She retrieved some clay bowls from a shelf nearby and began ladling stew into each of them.

"Ah, it's ready!" Helen said brightly. "Thank you, Sophia! Now, if everyone could take a seat at the table," she gestured to a large wooden table pushed up against the wall, "we can start talking about that no-good priest who's taken over our temple. I'm not sure how your mother got tangled up with him, Milly, dear, but—"

"He kidnapped her," Milly interjected, taking a bowl of stew from Sophia and trying to keep her voice steady. "At least... I think he did."

Helen clicked her tongue sympathetically and sat down at the table with the others. "I'm so sorry to hear that," she said gently. "Come, child. Tell us your story."

Milly slid into a seat across from Helen, nestled between Ashley and Wolfstan. The warmth of the stew seeped into her hands, offering comfort. As the others looked at her expectantly, waiting patiently to hear what she had to say, she felt an unexpected sense of ease.

The characters she'd spent months getting to know through her computer screen had become real friends. And Ashley and Lucy—well, they would be her friends forever.

"Most of you already know the story," Milly began, as Sophie set a basket of bread down in the centre of the table. "So... my mum has been missing for months. One day, I found Athena's Shawl in her closet—though I didn't know what it was at the time." She dipped a piece of bread into her stew. The broth burned her tongue, but it was still one of the best things she'd ever tasted. "I accidentally activated the shawl while playing my favourite computer game—"

"We still don't know what a computer game is," Wolfstan interrupted. "What's a computer?"

"Uh..." Milly hesitated, unsure how to explain something as technologically advanced as a computer to someone from mediaeval times. "Well, it's kind of like..."

"It's basically a metal machine shaped like a box," Lucy said, tearing into her lamb stew. "And you can play games on it by pressing different buttons."

"Right…" Wolfstan replied, scratching his head. "I suppose I'll just have to pretend I understand. Go on, Milly."

Milly launched into the story, recounting how Louie fell into Athena's Shawl. She explained how she had followed him, only to find herself trapped in the world of the game she'd been playing just seconds earlier. "This lady with a fruit basket led us to the temple," she said. "She told us the priest could help me find my mum. But then Louie must have smelled my mum's necklace on him, because he started grabbing at his robes, and—wouldn't you know it—out fell the exact necklace my mum was wearing the day she went missing."

She took another bite of stew and fished a piece of lamb meat out of her bowl for Louie, who was lying under the table at her feet, whimpering slightly as she recounted the tale. "Then, my sister and brother showed up and took me back home," she continued. "I was pretty angry with them at first, but I understand why they did it. And… now I'm back, and I've brought Ashley and Lucy with me."

The group listened in silence, nodding solemnly as they finished their bowls of stew.

Suddenly, King Jason slammed his bowl down on the table a little too aggressively, making Milly jump. "And you didn't think to bring Athena's Shawl with you?" he scoffed, wiping his moustache with the hem of his robe. "I suppose I can't put too much blame on you. You're just a stupid girl."

"Don't you dare call her stupid!" Ashley snapped, glaring at King Jason. "Milly is putting her life on the line to save her mum, and all you care about is getting your hands on Athena's Shawl! Isn't that right, *Your*

Majesty?" She emphasised the title mockingly, making Milly smile. Ashley always had her back.

"I don't know how I was supposed to bring Athena's Shawl with me," Milly said through gritted teeth. "We still don't know much about it, remember? It works as a portal, sure, but if I'm going into Athena's Shawl, I don't know how I can also take it with me. Besides, my sister has the bottom-right corner anyway—"

"Easy, Milly," Mirabel interrupted gently. "We don't blame you for not knowing how to bring Athena's Shawl with you. The king himself probably wouldn't know how to do that." She glanced at King Jason, who was staring into his empty bowl, looking slightly ashamed. "You mustn't be too hard on Milly, Your Majesty," she told him. "Her mother is missing, and she's only just learned to wield Athena's Shawl. She must be feeling quite overwhelmed."

"I wouldn't say I even fully know how to wield it," Milly admitted with a shrug. "I'm lucky it worked this time around. I wasn't sure it would. Although, if the sun hadn't been out, we could probably have just used my brother's nightlight…"

"What's a nightlight?" Faramund asked.

Milly shook her head and turned to Helen, who had been quietly listening to her story from across the table. "Anyway… that's basically what happened. I don't know why Deimos Asgard has my mother, or what he plans to do with her. All I know is that I have to save her."

"I see," Helen said, pressing her lips into a thin line. "I'm so sorry you've had to go through this, Milly. I can't say I can offer much assistance… but you've got four fierce warriors ready to fight for you." She gestured toward Catalina, Mirabel, Wolfstan, and Faramund. "So, I believe you'll find your mother. Trust in your friends and believe in yourself."

King Jason sighed dramatically. "I suppose that doesn't include me?" he asked. "I have a sword, you know. I can fight, too."

"Oh, of course," Helen said, her tone lightly patronising. "And what a great swordsman you are!"

Milly stifled a giggle as Faramund and the others burst into hearty laughter. Sophia quietly cleared their bowls, then placed a basket of honey cakes on the table.

"Ah, lovely!" Helen said, helping herself to a cake. "Thank you, Sophia. Now, sit down with us, my child. You've done more than enough."

Sophia joined them, selecting a honey cake from the basket and nibbling on it, clearly pleased to be included in the gathering.

Milly, sharing a cake with Ashley, turned to Catalina. "So," she began. "Earlier, you mentioned the priest has a secret." She bit into her half of the honey cake, the sweet, citrusy flavour melting in her mouth. "My goodness," she said, addressing Sophia. "This is absolutely delicious."

"'This is absolutely delicious,'" Lucy mimicked in a sing-song voice. "You sound like Mary Poppins." She took a bite of her cake, her eyes widening. "You're not wrong, though."

Catalina smiled at the exchange before focusing on Milly. "While you were gone, we uncovered something very interesting about Deimos Asgard—'Deacon Alexiou,' as he calls himself." She paused to swallow a bite of her honey cake. "We think we can use this secret against him, especially with Athena's Shawl on your side."

"Okay," Milly said, leaning in. "What's his secret?"

Catalina's expression grew serious as the room quieted. "Deimos Asgard is not who he claims to be," she began. "He's not just a priest. He possesses an ancient artifact—a forbidden amulet that grants him

92

dark powers. This amulet is the source of his influence and his control over Athena's Shawl."

Milly's eyes widened. "So the amulet is his weakness? If we can take it from him, he'll lose his power?"

Mirabel nodded. "Exactly. The amulet is his Achilles' heel. If we can destroy it, we'll weaken him significantly. But it won't be easy. We don't even know where he keeps it."

"Did you find out where my mother is?" Milly asked urgently.

Catalina sighed. "Unfortunately, her exact location remains a mystery. But we do have an idea. Don't get your hopes up too high, but—"

"Where?" Milly interrupted, leaning forward. "Where is she?"

"We believe she's somewhere in a castle on the outskirts of the next village—the one beyond the forest," Wolfstan said. "It'll take time to get there, but we've been spying on Deimos Asgard, and that appears to be where he lives."

"How soon can we leave?" Milly asked, standing abruptly. "What are we waiting for? My mum could be in serious danger!"

"Slow down, Milly," Mirabel said gently. "Before we do anything, we need to find and destroy Deimos Asgard's amulet. We suspect it's hidden somewhere deep within the temple, but we can't be sure."

"That would be the best place to start," Catalina agreed. "Let's come up with a plan, shall we?"

The group huddled together, their heads close as they strategised. Though Milly felt the weight of urgency pressing on her, she knew they needed a solid plan. Catalina reached into her robes and pulled out a tattered map. She spread it on the table and traced a route with her finger.

"Exploring the temple will be dangerous," Catalina said. "But we've handled our share of dungeons before. With any luck, we'll find the amulet quickly. Once it's destroyed, we can make our way to the castle where Deimos Asgard is keeping your mother."

The group nodded in agreement, their determination solidifying as they prepared for the journey ahead.

King Jason, who had been quietly observing, spoke up. "We should split into two groups. One group will infiltrate the temple and locate the amulet, while the other group remains on standby. Once the amulet is destroyed, we'll head straight to the castle and rescue your mother."

Milly nodded, appreciating the logic in his plan. "Who should go to the temple, and who should stay behind?"

Captain Catalina considered the question for a moment. "I'll lead the group to the temple — Mirabel, Wolfstan, Milly, and Ashley — you're with me." Louie barked excitedly, and she reached down to scratch him under his chin. "And you can come too, of course, Louie," she said with a grin. "Meanwhile, King Jason, Lucy, and Faramund will stay here as the backup team. Once we give the signal, head straight for the castle."

Lucy, Faramund, and King Jason exchanged determined glances. "We'll be ready," Lucy said. "We're going to save your mum, Milly. I just know it."

Before Milly could respond, the wall next to the smouldering fire pit began to ripple and swirl, its surface distorting like liquid. Milly's heart jumped — she knew instantly what it meant. "Oh," she said, pointing. "That's Fran and Charlie. Brace yourselves."

"What in the world?" Helen exclaimed, staring at the swirling wall with wide eyes. "I've never seen anything like this!"

94

Sure enough, Fran and Charlie tumbled through the portal a moment later. But what happened next caught Milly completely off guard. Harry, closely followed by Chris, fell through right behind them, landing in an awkward heap on the floor.

"What the—" Harry started as he scrambled to his feet, his eyes darting around the room. "Where are we?"

"Uh, hello?" Milly said, stepping forward to help him up. "What are you two doing here?"

"We stopped by your house to check on you," Harry said. Milly couldn't suppress a grin, even as she tried to remain stern. "We ran into Fran and Charlie," he continued, gesturing to her younger siblings. "They were messing around with some cloth, a framed picture of your parents, and a Spider-Man nightlight. Naturally, we thought, 'Well, that's weird,' and they decided to show us what they were doing."

"Which, apparently, was interdimensional travel?" Chris added, shooting Fran and Charlie a puzzled look. "Seriously, where did you guys bring us? This feels like an entirely different world."

Helen, who had been watching with a mix of confusion and concern, folded her arms. "Okay, what is going on? Who are you people, and why are you in my house?"

"They're with me," Milly said quickly, ushering Fran, Charlie, Harry, and Chris toward the door. "Just… give me a minute, okay?" She slipped outside with them and closed the door behind her.

Once they were in the garden, Milly turned to her siblings, arms crossed and fuming. "Fran!" she began. "I know you've figured out how to use Athena's Shawl, but you can't just—"

"You're not the only one who wants to rescue Mum," Fran interrupted, sticking out her lower lip in a pout. "And your friends were worried about you, so I brought them along. What's the big deal?"

95

Milly groaned, running her fingers through her hair. "Do you have any idea what Dad's going to think? He's going to figure out we stole Athena's Shawl, and we'll be lucky if he doesn't call the police!"

"Police?" Harry said, raising an eyebrow. "What are the police going to do in a situation like this?" He looked around at the garden, taking in the strange flowers and distant towers. "This place looks like something out of *War of the Ages 2*. And hey… wasn't that Captain Catalina in there? And King Jason?" He let out a laugh, shaking his head. "Man, this is something else."

"Harry," Milly said, exasperated. "This isn't a game. This is real. My mum is out there somewhere, and we're trying to save her."

Harry nodded, his expression softening. "I get that, Milly. And for what it's worth, we're here to help."

Fran crossed her arms and gave Milly a determined look. "We all are."

Milly sighed, torn between frustration and gratitude. "Fine," she said after a moment. "But no more surprises, okay? Let's figure this out together."

"You've got that right," Chris said, standing on his tiptoes to peer through the open window. "Did you bring Ashley and Lucy along with you, Milly?"

"I might have," Milly said, feeling a bit self-conscious under Harry's gaze. "So what? Maybe they can help me find my mum."

"Why would your mum be here?" Harry asked, scratching the back of his head. "How do you ever know she's here?"

"Because Louie found her necklace," Milly explained, her tone edging toward impatience. She was growing tired of repeating herself. "We think my mum was kidnapped by an evil priest. If you're that curious, ask Captain Catalina. She might even have a job for you — I don't know."

"Okay…" Harry said, nodding slowly. "Well, I'm happy to help however I can. If your mum's really here, then finding her is the most important thing."

Milly gave him a small smile. "Thank you. I appreciate it."

"So… where are we, exactly?" Chris asked. "Fran told us that weird white cloth of yours could transport us to the world of *War of the Ages 2*. Is that true?"

"That's… pretty much the case," Milly said. "I know it sounds crazy, but I think my mum must be connected to Athena's Shawl somehow."

"That explains why you were asking us about Athena's Shawl the other day at lunch," Harry said, slapping his palm to his forehead. "You should've just told us what was going on, Milly! We'd have tried to help you, you know?"

"Really?" Milly felt her cheeks flush.

"Of course," Harry said.

Fran suddenly tugged at the back of Milly's school uniform. "Um… are you mad at Charlie and me?" she asked, her voice small. "We just wanted to help… I'm sorry."

Milly sighed, realising that everyone who had fallen through the portal was now a part of this unexpected adventure. "Look, Fran, I appreciate that you want to help, but this is dangerous," she said, softening her tone. "And Dad is going to be furious when he finds out we went into Athena's Shawl without permission."

"We don't mean to get in the way," Fran said, slipping her arm around Charlie's shoulder. "We're just worried about Mum. Besides, you kind of need us. You forgot to bring a piece of the cloth and Mum and Dad's picture with you." She patted her school bag, which Milly now noticed for the first time. "Luckily, I brought them. We'll need them if we want to go back."

"Oh…" Milly blinked, realising Fran was right. "Bless you, Fran. Admittedly, I'm not the best at thinking things through."

"I know," Fran said, smirking. "That's why we're here."

Milly chuckled, then nodded. "Alright. Let's go inside and talk to Captain Catalina. It can't hurt to have more people helping us, right? Just promise me you'll be careful," she said, fixing both of her siblings with a stern look.

"We will!" Charlie said, practically bouncing with excitement. "We'll make sure to listen to you, Milly."

"We promise," Fran said, placing a hand over her heart. "Do you really think we can find Mum?"

Milly smiled, her determination evident. "I think so. Alright, then. Let's head back inside."

Chapter 8
The Trials of the Temple

C aptain Catalina wasn't exactly thrilled about Harry, Chris, Fran, and Charlie tagging along, but she understood they were only trying to help Milly. Much to Chris and Charlie's disappointment, Catalina had them stay behind with Faramund, King Jason, and Lucy. However, Harry and Fran were adamant about joining Milly and the others on the mission to the temple.

As the group trekked toward their destination, Mirabel took the opportunity to teach Ashley the basics of sword fighting — something Ashley had never imagined herself learning. "When we get there, we'll take out the guards, and you can grab one of their swords," Mirabel said. "Remember to focus on your stance and posture, your footwork, and how to manoeuvre. You'll need to decide when to thrust, slash, or block."

Ashley's anxious expression betrayed her nerves. "I've never used a sword before. I did a little fencing when I was a kid, but that was ages ago…"

"Don't worry," Mirabel reassured her. "I'll guide you when the time comes. Just think of the sword as an extension of yourself. Work with it, not against it."

Meanwhile, Wolfstan was coaching Milly on the art of archery. Milly wasn't entirely new to it, though her experience was limited to the training targets at archery camp. She'd never hit a bullseye, but Wolfstan seemed confident in her abilities.

"One of the guards will likely have a bow," he told her. "It might be a bit large for you, but you'll manage."

"I hope so," Milly replied, glancing back at Harry and Fran, who were lagging behind. "What about Fran and Harry?"

99

"Yeah, what about me?" Harry chimed in. "I might not be the sharpest, but I can fight. Do I get a sword?"

"Grab one from a guard — if there are any left," Catalina said, her tone a mix of amusement and exasperation. "Your main job, though, is to protect that little girl." She nodded toward Fran, who was clearly tiring from the walk.

"Yeah, Harry," Milly teased. "You've babysat Fran before, haven't you? Think of this as the ultimate babysitting gig."

Harry rolled his eyes. "Well, I'm not getting paid for it this time, am I?" With a resigned sigh, he turned to Fran. "Alright, come on." He hoisted her onto his shoulders, and she happily rode piggyback the rest of the way to the temple.

The temple loomed ahead, shrouded in fog and heavily guarded. Despite its peaceful appearance, Louie whimpered at the sight of it, and Milly felt a pang of unease. She couldn't help but think about the statues they had encountered before. Had they destroyed ancient guardians of the temple? Though the statues had attacked them, the idea of causing such a disturbance felt like tempting fate. Perhaps they had freed the guardians from their stone prisons — but it was impossible to know for sure.

Milly, Catalina, Ashley, Mirabel, Harry, Fran, and Louie approached the temple's entrance, while Wolfstan positioned himself behind a large stump, his sleep arrows at the ready. Catalina distracted the guards with casual conversation, giving Wolfstan the opportunity to take them out one by one. Each guard crumpled to the ground, sound asleep.

Milly, Ashley, and Harry set about searching the unconscious guards for weapons. Ashley claimed a long sword from a female guard, while Harry opted for the head guard's greatsword. Milly eventually found a bow strapped to the back of a smaller guard, along with a quiver full of arrows. She grinned, holding up her prize. "Perfect!"

She turned to Captain Catalina, who stood watch over the group. "Alright, Captain. We're ready."

Catalina nodded. "Okay, everyone. Remember to stay silent while we're in the temple. That includes you, Louie."

Louie let out a small whine but seemed to understand. He sat down, wagging his tail and panting softly. Captain Catalina smiled briefly before her expression turned serious again. "I don't know what sort of challenges lie ahead, but the quieter we are, the better."

With that, she motioned for Milly and the others to follow her into the temple.

The moment they stepped inside, the group became painfully aware of their footsteps echoing against the brick floor and reverberating off the stone columns. Milly and Ashley instinctively began walking on tiptoes, while Harry hoisted Fran onto his shoulders again to minimize the noise.

From the outside, the temple had appeared modest in size, but once they moved past the chamber where they had encountered Deimos Asgard, they discovered a winding staircase that spiralled down into a labyrinth of narrow tunnels and dimly lit chambers. The maze-like complexity was overwhelming, even for Captain Catalina, but it was Harry who seemed the most affected.

"I feel like the walls are closing in on me," he said hoarsely, crouching low to the ground. "Fran, I need you to get down, just for a minute."

Fran slid off his shoulders as Harry lowered himself to sit on the cold, dusty floor. His breathing was shallow, and his hands trembled slightly.

Milly knelt beside him, placing a tentative hand over his. "Hey," she whispered. "Are you okay? What can I do to help?"

Before Harry could answer, Louie trotted over and nudged his arm with his wet nose. Then, much to Milly's surprise — and slight horror — Louie jumped up and gave Harry a slobbery kiss on the cheek.

Harry let out a shaky laugh, squeezing Milly's hand and pulling Louie into a hug. "I'll... I'll be okay," he stammered. "I'm just not great with small spaces." He took a few deep breaths, his grip on Milly's hand steadying.

Catalina glanced back, her brow furrowed. "I'm sorry," she said, her voice softening. "But we can't stay here too long. We have to keep moving."

Mirabel shot her a sharp look. "Take it easy, Captain. He's just a kid." She knelt down next to Harry, her tone gentler now. "Hey, I used to be afraid of tight spaces, too. It's not easy to deal with, but you're not alone, okay?"

Harry nodded, his breathing beginning to even out. "Thanks," he said quietly. After a moment, he scratched Louie behind the ears one last time before pushing himself to his feet. "Let's go. I'll be fine."

Catalina nodded. "Alright. Let's keep moving."

The group pressed on, navigating the winding tunnels until they emerged into a massive, dome-shaped chamber. The room was a stark contrast to the suffocating corridors, but the air felt heavy, almost oppressive.

Dim light filtered through cracks in the walls, illuminating intricate carvings etched into the stone. The designs caught Milly's and Ashley's attention immediately, the ancient symbols both mesmerising and enigmatic.

Their awe was short-lived. A skittering noise echoed from above, sharp and rhythmic.

Everyone froze.

From the ceiling, enormous spiders — each the size of a hackney carriage — began to descend. Their hairy legs stretched outward as they clicked their massive fangs together menacingly.

Louie erupted into frantic barking, startling Milly so much that she dropped his leash. Fran screamed and clung to Milly's elbow, trembling as the first spider landed heavily on the ground.

Milly's heart raced. She tried to scream, but no sound came out. The sheer sight of the monstrous arachnids made her blood run cold.

Wolfstan nudged her gently. "You alright?"

Milly nodded faintly, though her shaking hands betrayed her fear. She reached for the bow she'd taken from the guard at the temple entrance, fumbling slightly as she readied an arrow.

Captain Catalina unsheathed her throwing knives, her voice commanding. "Prepare yourselves! We've got company."

Harry, still pale from his earlier panic, gripped his great sword tightly. He took a step forward, pointing the blade at a particularly grotesque spider.

Mirabel and Ashley readied their weapons as well, their faces tense but determined.

The spiders descended one by one, their glistening eyes reflecting the dim light. The air seemed to thicken as the creatures began to encircle the group.

Milly forced herself to steady her breathing. She had faced terrifying challenges before — and she was so close to rescuing her mother. She couldn't falter now.

Taking a deep breath, she notched her arrow and prepared to fight.

One of the spiders lunged toward Milly, its glistening fangs aimed right at her. Reacting on pure instinct, she fumbled with trembling hands to notch an arrow. Drawing back the bowstring, she aimed for its enormous head.

Twang!

The arrow flew, striking the spider's hairy body. It wasn't a perfect hit, but it was enough to make the creature screech in pain. Milly froze as it kept coming, its legs skittering closer. Panic seized her, and she let out a hoarse cry.

"H-help!"

Before she could react further, Louie leapt into action. With a fierce growl, he lunged onto the spider's back, sinking his teeth into its neck. The spider let out one final, agonizing screech before collapsing in front of her.

Breathing heavily, Milly crouched next to Louie and hugged him briefly. "Good boy," she whispered, her voice shaky but grateful. Fuelled by adrenaline, she straightened up, notching another arrow. Her little sister Fran cowered behind her, and Milly's determination only grew. She would protect Fran no matter what.

To her left, Wolfstan moved like a shadow, his arrows flying with deadly precision. Each one hit its mark, bringing spiders down with cold efficiency. Mirabel charged into the fray with her sword, her strikes swift and decisive as she felled several spiders at once.

Captain Catalina darted between the creatures, throwing knives with surgical accuracy. Every blade she hurled found a weak spot, bringing another monstrous spider to the ground.

Harry, regaining his composure, wielded his great sword with growing confidence. "Take this!" he yelled, stabbing a spider through the abdomen. Its legs flailed briefly before it fell lifeless at his feet.

Even Ashley was holding her own, mimicking Mirabel's movements. She focused on slicing the spiders' legs, hobbling them before finishing them off.

The room was filled with the clash of weapons, the terrified cries of the group, and the high-pitched squeals of the spiders. The cacophony was overwhelming, the battle relentless, but the team fought with everything they had.

Finally, Milly found herself facing the largest spider of them all. It loomed over her, its multiple eyes gleaming with malice. Heart pounding, she took a deep breath and steadied her shaking hands. Drawing her bowstring back as far as it would go, she lost an arrow that struck the spider in its abdomen.

It screeched in agony but didn't fall. Milly took a step back, unsure what to do, but Mirabel stepped in, her sword slicing cleanly through its body in a single, powerful stroke.

The spider crumpled to the floor, its legs twitching before it went still.

For a moment, the room was silent except for their heavy breathing.

Captain Catalina surveyed the scene, wiping her knives clean. She smiled at the younger members of the group. "Well done, everyone. We make quite the team."

Fran turned to Milly, her eyes wide with admiration. "You were amazing, Milly. I know how much you hate spiders."

Milly managed a shaky laugh, still catching her breath. "I guess that's what motivated me," she admitted.

She looked at the grotesque, lifeless bodies of the spiders scattered around the room and shivered. She couldn't believe she had stood her ground. It was the bravest thing she had ever done, and she knew it was thanks to the courage of her friends fighting alongside her.

Wanting to put as much distance as possible between themselves and the spiders, Milly straightened up, brushing dust off her skirt. "Let's keep moving," she said, her voice stronger now. "I have a feeling, giant spiders aren't the worst thing lurking in this temple."

Fran clung to her arm, and Louie stayed close by, his tail wagging slightly as if to reassure her. Together, the group pressed forward into the unknown.

~

As they ventured deeper into the temple, Milly and the others came across a rather peculiar sight — a set of three marble doorways, each decorated with ancient symbols and guarded by strange-looking statues. Milly approached the door closest to her, her curiosity piqued. The symbols on the door seemed to tell some sort of story, but their meaning eluded her completely. Captain Catalina examined the symbols thoughtfully.

"This temple is full of challenges, and each door leads to a different trial," she said. "We must choose wisely."

Fran, still awestruck by Milly's show of bravery in the room with the spiders, pointed to the second doorway. "Maybe that one?" she suggested. "There aren't any symbols that look like snakes on it, so I vote that one." The rest of the group stared at her in disbelief. "What?" she said. "If there are giant spiders here, there are definitely giant snakes lurking about somewhere." She held onto Milly's arm. Fran hated snakes just as much as Milly hated spiders. "I just know it," she said.

"I think we should go that way," Wolfstan said, pointing to the door furthest away from them. "That symbol looks like a glass of wine," he gestured to a goblet-shaped etching on the door. "Perhaps there's a great feast waiting for us, should we make the right decision."

"I don't know…" Catalina said, arching an eyebrow. "That feels like a trap."

"Well, I'm sure each challenge is equally horrible," Harry said, folding his arms across his chest. "So, it doesn't really matter, does it?"

After some back and forth, the group reached a consensus, and — much to Wolfstan's dismay — decided to enter the second doorway. Milly pushed the cold marble door open, and after walking for a while, they found themselves in a room filled with mirrors of all shapes and sizes.

"It's a maze of mirrors," Mirabel said, stating the obvious. "Stay close, everyone. We don't want to get separated."

They clasped hands and walked in a single-file line, Milly taking the lead since she had to hold onto Louie's leash, and Mirabel taking up the rear. Slowly but surely, they made their way through the maze, their own distorted reflections sometimes leading them astray. All the while, they could hear faint laughter echoing throughout the mirrored walls. The laughter grew louder, and at the end of the maze, a mysterious figure stood in front of a great door. Milly couldn't help but gasp. It was a monster with the body of a lion, the wings of a bird, and the head of a beautiful woman.

"Uh… What is that?" Milly asked, stopping in her tracks.

Captain Catalina let go of Milly's hand and took a few steps forward. "Try to stay calm," she said to the group. "It's a Sphinx."

"Okay… and what's that exactly?" Milly stared at the monster. It didn't seem like it wanted to harm them… not yet, anyway. It was just standing in front of the door, laughing that horrible laugh.

"I read a book that had a Sphinx in it once," Ashley said, looking reproachfully at the strange creature. "The characters had to answer her riddle to get past the door she was guarding. The problem was, if they got the answer wrong… the Sphinx said that she was going to kill and eat them."

"I don't like this," Fran said, clinging to Harry's arm.

"Ah, the Sphinx," Wolfstan said, taking out his bow and arrow. "A fascinating beast, really —"

"That's not going to work, Wolfstan," Mirabel said. "She's an immortal being. You can't kill her."

"Hmm," he thought for a moment and grabbed one of the last remaining sleep arrows out of his quiver. "Do you think I could put her to sleep? Unless you feel up to solving some convoluted riddle, that is." Without waiting for Mirabel's answer, Wolfstan shot the sleep arrow at the Sphinx. The creature swiped the arrow out of the air — much like a cat swipes at an unsuspecting bird — and stomped it into the ground, promptly breaking it in half.

"Oh…" Wolfstan lowered his bow. "Uh… maybe that wasn't the best idea."

"Oh, for God's sake," Captain Catalina said, walking towards the Sphinx. "I'm sure if we put our heads together, we can figure out the answer to her riddle. How hard could it be?" Milly and the others followed her, feeling wary but unsure of what else they could do to get past this particular beast.

Up close, the Sphinx was simultaneously majestic and terrifying. Louie began to growl, the hairs on his back standing stiffly upright. Milly hushed him and tightened her grip on his leash. "It's okay, boy," she murmured, reaching down to scratch his head. "There's nothing to be afraid of."

In truth, Milly was deeply unnerved by the Sphinx. The creature's hair was as dark as the night sky, her lips painted a vivid crimson. Her massive, slightly withered grey wings contrasted sharply with her muscled lioness body, making her appearance both striking and unsettling. As they drew closer, the Sphinx flicked her tail, and her eerie laughter abruptly ceased. A smile spread across her lips, and she addressed them in a syrupy voice:

"If you wish to pass, you must solve my riddle. Are you up for the challenge, or will you turn back and live another day?"

"Speak your riddle, Sphinx," Catalina said firmly. "We only ask that you give us enough time to figure out the answer."

"Naturally," the Sphinx replied. "You may take as much time as you need. Answer carefully, though... because you only get one try." She folded her wings and sat gracefully before the great marble door. "Here is your riddle:

'I'm long in the beginning, and the end as well. I'm short in the middle — why, you ask? Time will tell. You won't see me at night or in a dark room, But if you're lucky, you might find me on the surface of the moon. What am I?'"

"A crater!" Harry blurted out immediately. "Because craters can be short or long, and you can find them on the surface of the moon. Right?" He grinned at Catalina, who looked as though she was fighting the urge to throttle him.

"Harry..." Milly shook her head. "Come on."

"That is not our final answer," Catalina said quickly to the Sphinx, who responded with a shrill laugh. Turning to the group, she glared at Harry. "I'll do the talking. Okay?"

"Er… sorry," Harry mumbled, looking sheepish. Louie licked the back of his hand, and Harry bent down to pet him. "Well… do you guys have any other ideas about what the answer could be?"

"Let me think for a moment," Mirabel said, frowning in concentration. "'I'm long in the beginning, and the end as well. I'm short in the middle — why, you ask? Time will tell.' So… it must have something to do with time or something affected by time."

"Doesn't time affect everything?" Wolfstan muttered. "Way to narrow it down, Mirabel."

"You could help instead of being a sarcastic twit," Mirabel snapped, crossing her arms. Running her fingers through her hair, she sighed deeply. "Okay, so… the rest of the riddle says, 'You won't see me at night or in a dark room,' so it's probably something related to light as well."

"Like Athena's Shawl," Milly said. "You need light to activate it… and you can't see light in a dark room because there is none."

"So, then… is 'light' the answer?" Fran asked.

"I don't think so," Mirabel replied. "Light isn't 'long in the beginning and the end as well'… whatever that means."

"The beginning of what?" Ashley asked, sitting cross-legged on the floor as she rubbed her temples. Louie plopped into her lap and closed his eyes. "The end of what?"

"The Sphinx is being purposefully vague," Catalina said. "I think you're on the right track, though, Mirabel. We need to break the riddle apart and solve it bit by bit. Then we'll have a better chance of figuring out the answer." She lowered herself to the floor beside Ashley, stroking

Louie's fur as the dog dozed. Milly and Fran joined them, forming a small circle. Catalina continued, "Let's say the riddle refers to the beginning, middle, and end of a day. That seems like a reasonable starting point. Can you think of anything that's long at the start of the day, short in the middle, and long again at the end?"

The group sat in contemplative silence for several minutes. Fran cradled her head in her hands, while Mirabel pursed her lips in thought. Ashley, seemingly lost in her own musings, rested a hand on Louie's back.

"Milly?" Ashley said suddenly, breaking the quiet. "Do you remember that history lesson we had at the beginning of the school year? It was really nice out, so Mr Hayes let us have class outside?"

"Kind of," Milly replied, wondering where this was leading. "I can't say I remember the actual lesson all that well... but it was a fun class."

"It was," Ashley agreed. "Mr Hayes brought us jam doughnuts, and we spent ages laughing about how tall our shadows were."

Milly gave her a confused look. "Um, Ash? While I appreciate the trip down memory lane, I'm not sure what this has to do with the Sphinx's riddle."

"I'm getting there," Ashley said, raising a finger. "Milly, what time of day do we have history class?"

"The crack of dawn, it feels like," Harry interjected, having overheard the conversation. "What are you two blithering on about school for?"

"We have history first thing in the morning," Milly said, beginning to catch on to Ashley's train of thought. "Our shadows were tall in the morning."

"Exactly," Ashley said, nodding. "And at lunchtime, we looked at our shadows again and noticed they were really short, remember?"

"That's it!" Mirabel exclaimed, clapping her hands as she leapt to her feet. Louie jolted awake in Ashley's lap and barked sharply, not wanting to miss out on the excitement. "I can't believe I didn't think of this before. In the morning, the rising sun makes your shadow long. The same thing happens in the evening when the sun sets. At noon, though, the sun's rays fall vertically, and our shadows are short." She spoke so quickly that Milly could barely keep up.

"Slow down, Mirabel," Catalina said. "So... you think the answer could be 'a shadow'? Does that fit the rest of the riddle?"

"It does!" Mirabel said confidently. "You can't see a shadow at night or in a dark room, can you? And Harry was actually onto something earlier — the moon's craters cast shadows. That must be the answer."

"If you're certain..." Catalina said, rising from the floor. She strode over to the Sphinx and cleared her throat. "We have our final answer," she declared.

The Sphinx lifted her head lazily, her eyes narrowing. "Took you long enough," she said. "What do you think the answer is, my child? I hope, for your sake, that you're right."

"A shadow," Catalina said, her voice steady but her hands wringing nervously. Milly had never seen her so tense before; Catalina was usually the epitome of composure. "That's the answer."

The Sphinx paused, her expression unreadable. Then, a wide smile spread across her face. "Well done," she said. "I have travelled with my master, to serve him in this place, and he won't be pleased... but there's nothing I can do about that now. You may pass." She stepped aside and bowed her head, allowing the group to enter through the great marble doorway.

"Nice work, Mirabel," Catalina said. "Brilliant thinking!"

"Well, Ashley deserves the credit," Mirabel said, patting Ashley on the back. "I wouldn't have solved it without her!"

Ashley flushed crimson. "Oh, come on. You'd have figured it out eventually."

"Seriously, Ash. That was amazing," Milly said, grinning.

Ashley smiled, standing a little taller as they entered a small room filled with heaps of... jewellery? "This is what she was guarding?" Ashley asked, picking up a golden necklace adorned with a ruby pendant. "Huh."

"This is incredible," Wolfstan said, his eyes gleaming. "We're going to be rich!"

"Hold on," Catalina said, grabbing his arm before he could dive headfirst into the glittering hoard. "We're here for a reason. This could be where Deimos Asgard is keeping his amulet."

"I certainly hope so," Mirabel said, glancing around the room. "This has been quite the ordeal."

The group searched for several minutes, sifting through piles of gold and silver jewellery. Milly kept an eye out for anything that seemed vaguely "amulet-like," though she wasn't entirely sure what she was looking for, which made the task challenging.

"What does the amulet look like?" she asked. "I know you lot said you were spying on him, but... did he mention anything about its actual appearance?"

"Nope," Wolfstan replied. "But it's probably going to stand out from everything else in here, right? Deimos Asgard must have had the Sphinx hide it for a reason. Even if someone solved her riddle, Asgard would want his precious amulet to be pretty hard to find—"

"Is that it?" Fran interrupted, pointing to something on the other side of the room.

It was another statue of Athena, and from its neck hung a dark purple amulet.

"An amulet is like a necklace, right?"

"Oh. Well, that was easy," Wolfstan remarked.

"That's got to be it," Catalina said, leaping and bounding over the heaps of jewellery towards the statue. "Now, all we have to do is figure out how to destroy it."

She carefully lifted the amulet from the statue's neck, turned it over in her hands a few times, and then slipped it into her pocket.

Chapter 9
Athena's Shawl

A few hours later, Milly and the others stood in front of a grand castle. The journey had been long and arduous, but after everything they'd endured, it was nothing they couldn't handle. Even Fran had managed to walk the entire way, which made Milly proud. They joined King Jason, Faramund, Charlie, Lucy, and Chris a few metres from the entrance. The group were clearly relieved to see their friends emerge from the temple unscathed.

"What was it like?" Chris asked Harry. "And where did you get that sword?"

"You had to be there, mate," Harry said, unsheathing his great sword. "Yeah, it's a beauty, isn't it?"

"I'm still upset I didn't get to go with you," Charlie grumbled, stomping his foot. "It's not fair."

"Oh, Charlie… you're too little," Milly said gently. "You can come on the next adventure. How does that sound?"

Meanwhile, Ashley was catching Lucy up on everything that had happened. "It was bonkers," she said. "I wish you'd been there, Lucy!"

"Me too…" Lucy replied, glancing at Faramund and King Jason. "But those blokes aren't so bad. We've come up with a plan for storming the castle."

Just then, Catalina clapped her hands, calling everyone to gather around. "Come on, then! Let's go over how we're going to do this—"

"We've got a plan!" Lucy chimed in. "Faramund and I will distract the guards while Charlie sneaks in through one of the windows—he's the only one small enough to fit. Once inside, he can let us in through the main entrance."

"That might just work," Catalina said, nodding. "Alright. Mirabel, Milly, Fran, and Wolfstan—you're with me. Harry, I'll need you to fend off any guards if necessary. Think you can handle that with that impressive sword of yours?"

Harry brandished his sword and gave a confident smile. "You can count on me."

"King Jason," Catalina said, turning to the weary-looking king, "you, Ashley, and Chris will act as lookouts. If the guards call for reinforcements or anything unusual happens, give us a signal, alright?"

King Jason and Ashley nodded.

"How's this?" Chris asked, cupping his hands around his mouth. "'Caw-CAW, Caw-CAW!'"

Ashley burst out laughing. "What a signal!"

"Brilliant," Catalina said with a smile. "Keep it down for now, though. Hopefully, you won't need to do anything, but I'll feel better knowing you're keeping watch."

The group moved cautiously towards the castle. Milly's heart pounded in her chest, but she refused to let her anxiety take over. *Be strong,* she told herself. *Be brave. You're so close to rescuing Mum.*

"Alright, let's go over the plan one more time," Catalina said, her sharp eyes scanning the castle's front entrance. "Faramund and Lucy, you'll handle the guards. Charlie, remember to be stealthy. Take Louie with you—he'll keep you safe."

Milly handed Charlie Louie's leash. The dog jumped up on Charlie, licking his face enthusiastically, clearly delighted.

"And Harry," Catalina continued, "you're our frontline defence. Milly, Mirabel, Fran, and Wolfstan, stay close to me. Together, we'll find Deimos Asgard and put an end to his evil once and for all."

"How are we going to destroy the amulet?" Milly asked.

To her surprise, Catalina shrugged. "It looks quite breakable to me," she said. "But honestly, I'm not sure." She took the amulet from her pocket, running her fingers over its gleaming purple jewel. "You can feel the power radiating from it—it's incredible."

"Destroying it may not be as simple as it seems," Wolfstan warned. "Who knows what might happen if we mishandle a magical artefact like that?"

"You're right," Catalina agreed, snapping out of her trance. "We'll proceed with caution and figure out the safest way to do this. Now, come on, everyone! This way."

While Faramund and Lucy distracted the guards — with Harry waiting around the corner in case their plan went awry — the rest of the group huddled near a side door, just out of view of the guards at the castle entrance.

"There," Captain Catalina whispered, pointing to a nearby window. "Do you think you can fit through that, Charlie?"

Charlie nodded. "I might need a bit of help getting up there. Can someone give me a boost?"

Wolfstan hoisted Charlie onto his shoulders, helping him climb through the small window. "Alright, Charlie, I'll hand Louie up to you next. Ready?"

"Uh-huh!" Charlie replied, his voice slightly muffled from behind the wall. Wolfstan carefully lifted Louie and passed him through the window. "Got him!" Charlie said, securing the dog in his arms. Moments later, the side door creaked open, and the group slipped into a spacious corridor, murmuring their praise for Charlie's bravery.

Charlie grinned as he bent down to hug Louie. "I know it was just for a second, but I'm glad Louie was with me," he said.

"You can keep walking him, if you like," Milly said. "Maybe you two can take care of each other."

"Okay!" Charlie beamed.

"Shhh!" Catalina pressed a finger to her lips. "We need to be quiet. There could be guards nearby."

They tiptoed through the corridor, with Catalina leading the way. After some time, they reached the base of a grand spiralling staircase. Catalina placed a hand on Milly's shoulder.

"We need to find the chamber where Deimos Asgard is holding your mum," she said softly.

Milly nodded, and the group began their ascent. At the top, a large black door loomed before them, its surface etched with sinister carvings. The sight of it made Milly's stomach churn.

"This must be it," she whispered, gripping Fran and Charlie's hands tightly.

Catalina kicked the door open, revealing a dark, foreboding chamber. Deimos Asgard stood in its centre, surrounded by swirling shadows. Milly's mother was confined in a glowing, magical cage. Milly froze in place.

"Mum!" she cried, dashing forward with Fran and Charlie in tow.

But Deimos Asgard murmured an incantation, and the floor beneath them turned viscous, like thick gelatine. Each step became a struggle, but Milly refused to stop. She *had* to reach her mother.

"Come on," she urged, dragging Fran and Charlie as Louie paddled desperately through the magical muck.

Deimos Asgard chuckled darkly. "Such determination," he sneered. "Foolish children! Did you truly believe you could defeat me?"

"Milly!" Louise Martin cried, gripping the bars of her cage. "Fran! Charlie! Be careful!"

Wolfstan fired arrows at the priest, but Deimos deflected each with a wave of his hand. Mirabel waded through the muck, trying to reach Milly and the others. "Hold on, children!" she called. "I'm coming to help you!"

Meanwhile, Catalina pulled the amulet from her pocket and held it aloft. "Release her, Asgard!" she demanded. "Or I'll destroy your precious amulet!"

Deimos Asgard laughed again, his hands tucked into the sleeves of his robes. His calm, mocking demeanour made Milly's blood run cold. "And how, exactly, do you plan to destroy it?"

Catalina's brow furrowed, and to Milly's surprise, she began slamming the amulet against the marble floor in desperation.

"That won't work," Asgard taunted, his voice sing-song. "Why not save yourself the trouble? Give the amulet to me, and I'll release the heir of Athena. She's been more trouble than she's worth—I've been eager to be rid of her."

"The heir of Athena?" Milly gasped, still struggling through the gelatinous floor. "What are you talking about?"

"You mean you don't know?" Asgard smirked. "Your mother is a distant heir of Athena, which is why she can wield the Shawl of Athena. And you, child, are an heir as well. That's how you and your sister have been able to use the shawl to travel between worlds so easily."

Milly's head sank beneath the floor's surface, and she fought her way back up, gasping for air. "What—" she sputtered, "what are you talking about?"

119

In a split second, she found herself lying flat on the cold marble. The floor had suddenly turned hard again. She helped Fran, Charlie, and Louie up, then turned to see a familiar face.

"Nemesis?" she said, rubbing her eyes.

The goddess was hovering in the air, her beautiful wings spread wide and her hair flowing majestically behind her. She was still wearing her blindfold — Milly guessed she never took it off — and appeared to be keeping Deimos Asgard in some sort of magical bind. He was struggling against an invisible force. Catalina, still clutching the amulet, was staring at Nemesis, wide-eyed.

"Ah… she's back!" Wolfstan exclaimed, notching another arrow on his bow. "We knew you'd return, goddess! But you're not getting your hands on the amulet or Athena's Shawl—"

"I'm not interested in either of those things," Nemesis interrupted, floating gracefully to the cage where Milly's mother was being held. "I am here to restore balance to the world."

With a snap of her fingers, she unlocked the cage and extended her hand to Milly's mother. "Come," she said. "Trust me. I will take you to your children."

Louise Martin hesitated briefly before taking her hand, and together they floated down to the floor.

"Kids!" she cried as Milly, Fran, and Charlie ran to her. "I'm so glad you're safe!" She enveloped them in a massive hug, tears streaming down her face.

Milly was crying too — she had waited for this moment for what felt like forever.

"Mum!" she sobbed. "We finally found you!"

"You did!" her mother said, holding them tightly. "I'm so proud of all of you!"

Louie barked happily and began running in circles around them.

"Louie! You came too!" Louise reached down to pet him, and he rolled onto his back for belly rubs. "Who's a good boy?"

"Now, Catalina..." Nemesis said, turning her attention to the young woman. "Let me see that amulet."

"N-no," Catalina stammered, her voice unusually high-pitched. "I... I don't want to give it up—"

Before she could finish, Nemesis snapped her fingers. The amulet crumbled to dust in Catalina's hands, the remnants slipping through her fingers like sand before vanishing entirely.

Catalina sighed. "Well... that's probably for the best, honestly."

"No!" Deimos Asgard bellowed. "Do you have any idea what you've done?" He fell to his knees as the shadows swirling around him dissipated. "Now I'll never be able to wield the power of Athena's Shawl!"

"That's rather the point," Nemesis said coolly. "You've had too much power for far too long, Deimos Asgard. It's time to restore balance to the world."

With another snap of her fingers, the evil priest found himself imprisoned in the same cage where Milly's mother had been held.

"How dare you!" Deimos Asgard shouted, pounding the metal bars with his fists. "This won't hold me forever, you know!"

"He's right," Nemesis said. "That cage is no longer imbued with the amulet's magic. You need to leave now!"

She turned to Louise Martin and took her hands. "Louise, you are the rightful owner of Athena's Shawl. Athena entrusted it to you, and you must keep it safe."

Louise nodded. "What will happen to the priest?"

Nemesis sighed. "Unfortunately, Deimos Asgard will always have a connection to Athena's Shawl. This probably won't be the last time you encounter him…"

She glanced at Deimos, who had stopped trying to escape. He folded his arms across his chest and tapped his foot impatiently.

"But for now, you're safe," Nemesis continued.

"We need to find Lucy, Ashley, Harry, and Chris," Milly said. "And— and say goodbye to everyone…"

A lump formed in her throat, and Mirabel pulled her into a tight hug.

"It's not goodbye forever," Mirabel said. "Your mother is the rightful owner of Athena's Shawl. That means you can visit us whenever you like."

She turned to Nemesis and bowed her head. "Thank you, Nemesis. And… we're sorry for, uh… taking you out earlier."

Nemesis smiled. "It's fine. You can't kill a goddess — you must have known that."

Mirabel nodded before turning to Milly, Fran, Charlie, and Louise. "I'll miss you all," she said, petting Louie on the head. "And I'll miss you too, boy!"

She glanced at Catalina, who was sitting on the ground, still in disbelief. Wolfstan was crouched beside her, trying to snap her out of it.

"They'll miss you too," Mirabel said. "And remember, you're always welcome here. We'll just have to, uh… explain to King Jason that he can't have Athena's Shawl. That'll be fun."

Milly picked up Louie's lead and took her mother's hand, giving Fran's a squeeze. "You still have the cloth and that picture of Mum and Dad, right, Fran?"

Fran nodded.

"Oh, your father!" Louise said, her face lighting up. "I can't believe I'm going to see him again. It's been far too long."

Milly smiled and took one last look at Mirabel and the others. "Let's go and find my friends," she said, her voice resolute. "And then… you know what to do."

Epilogue

When Milly climbed into her bed that night, she was absolutely knackered. Louie was fast asleep next to her pillow having had far too many of his favourite Louie chewies, and Ashley, Lucy, Harry, and Chris had gone home after having dinner with her family. As she began drifting off to sleep, she heard a soft knock at her bedroom door. Her mother and father let themselves in, and she couldn't help but think how wonderful it was to see them together again. Their family was whole once more. The hole that had been in her heart for so long had finally been mended.

"I know you're tired, darling," her mother said gently. "But we just wanted to say goodnight. You did a fantastic job today, and your dad and I are so incredibly proud of you." She leaned her head against John Martin's shoulder, her voice soft with emotion. "I've missed you all so much," she added. "It almost doesn't feel real to be home."

"I can't believe it either," Milly's father said. "You know, Louise… I should have had more faith in our kids. I was so worried about them going into that magical shawl. I didn't think it was safe. But Milly…" He leaned down and kissed his daughter's forehead. "You proved yourself today. You showed remarkable bravery, and I'll never be able to thank you enough for bringing your mum home."

Milly smiled, her gaze drifting to the window. Athena's Shawl was still hung up exactly where she'd left it, and the moonlight streaming through the fabric cast soft shadows of her parents dancing upon it.

"So… how did you come to have Athena's Shawl?" she asked, sitting up a little. "And does this mean I get to keep it?"

Her mother exchanged a glance with her husband, sighed, and then smiled. "We trust you," she said. "We can discuss it in the morning. Just promise to be careful, okay?"

"Okay," Milly said, reaching out to hug both her parents tightly. "Goodnight, Mum. Goodnight, Dad. I love you."

Her mother's eyes glistened in the moonlight. "We love you too, Milly," she said softly.

Printed in Great Britain
by Amazon

dc91df23-15a8-4832-8c97-b93286681a68R01